The
Intelligent
Warrior

STEVE JONES

The Intelligent Warrior

Command Personal Power with Martial Arts Strategies

Thorsons
An Imprint of HarperCollins*Publishers*
77–85 Fulham Palace Road,
Hammersmith, London W6 8JB

The website address is: www.thorsonselement.com

and *Thorsons* are trademarks of
HarperCollins*Publishers* Ltd

First published by Thorsons 2004

10 9 8 7 6 5 4 3 2 1

A catalogue record of this book is
available from the British Library

ISBN 0 00 716074 7

Printed and bound in Great Britain by
Martins The Printers Ltd, Berwick upon Tweed

contents

acknowledgements

I would like to thank the following for their help and support in the writing of this book: Susanna Abbot and the team at Thorsons, Michael Alcock, my mother and father, Master Sun Li, all those who have and who continue to study and train with me, Bruce Thomas, Grant Headley, The Gurdjieff Society, and a special thank you to Ria Holzerlandt and Dr Norman Jones.

This book is dedicated to the late Master Derek Jones

introduction

The purpose of this book is to provide a practical guide to using Martial Art strategies in everyday life; it aims to provide you with the necessary tools to analyse and transform areas in your life where fear and its related emotions operate. Central to the book is the concept of holistic self-defence, which is founded upon the principle that the primary form of intelligence to be applied to fear is one's sense of balance.

This book will also challenge many preconceived notions of what defines Martial Art. I examine many of the concepts and philosophies that comprise Martial Art and apply old wisdom to contemporary settings. I have personally found that the Chinese tradition (mainly derived from Taoism) is the closest in essence to true Martial Art and for this reason I have based the book primarily upon Chinese perspectives and spiritual backgrounds; however, this by no means excludes other cultural interpretations, nor is it meant to depreciate their teachings.

Having spent over 22 years studying Martial Art, I feel that its true roots and its place in our daily lives has been overlooked and, to a certain extent, forgotten. In the last 30 years, Martial Art has enjoyed an explosion of popularity and although popularity is generally a good thing, it has engendered a variety of erroneous perceptions and interpretations of what constitutes Martial Art. The need for an ego massage and the lure of easy money have led to the emergence of many an unscrupulous and misguided teacher, and the mass-media marketing of Martial Art has further confounded the problem by creating fantastic images and staging fight scenes that bear no resemblance to reality. All of this has brought the world of Martial Art to a crisis point – what was once a noble and valid path for self-evolution has become a vehicle for people seeking their own materialistic and egotistic ends. However, this is not all encompassing as I have met many good and true martial artists in my time who are distinguished from their inferior counterparts by the quality of their 'being' and not their chosen Martial Art style.

A Brief History of Kung Fu

As this book aims to interpret some of the original Martial Art precepts into contemporary life it would serve us well to briefly look at the roots of Kung Fu (a modern term generally describing Martial Art), for it is only by looking at its origins that we can begin to understand what its original purpose may have been. The Kung Fu tradition has a Chinese background and is inextricably linked with the spiritual teachings of Taoism. Central to the teaching of Taoism is the concept of the individual practitioner evolving a gradual harmonization with nature and the Tao (the life force that animates all things and can be found everywhere in the universe), and this is important because since its conception it has been clear that Kung Fu is about harmonization rather than domination.

The roots of Kung Fu are very difficult to trace through history, primarily because the practice dates back thousands of years, but the first writings on Chi Kung (a form of exercise that was the precursor to modern Kung Fu) date back to 3000 BC and have been subsequently added to and developed by a succession of extraordinary individuals. The Northern Shaolin Temple in China's Honan Province existed in approximately AD 580 and was the birthplace of modern Kung Fu. Legend dictates that Bodidharma, a Buddhist monk from India, travelled to China where he had been summoned to the court at Nanking. After a brief and not very successful trip, Bodidharma started his journey home, but before reaching his destination, he came upon the Shaolin Temple. The temple at that time was being used for scholarly Buddhist studies, and the monks were engaged in translating Buddhist scriptures from Sanskrit into Chinese. On meeting Bodidharma, the head monk refused him entry because his progressive Buddhist teachings placed less emphasis on scholarly pursuits than they did on more energetic forms of teaching. Bodidharma decided to wait outside in order to try to gain entry, and he is rumoured to have spent this time in intensive meditation. (There is some speculation as to how long he stayed there – some say 40 days, others say nine years, but I have it on fairly good authority that it was, in fact, three months.) During this time, many local people came to him for guidance, and word of Bodidharma's wisdom spread and finally found its way back to the temple. The head monk then conceded Bodidharma's superior knowledge and allowed him to enter the monastery (more fanciful accounts will say that Bodidharma drilled a hole in the wall with his stare). What Bodidharma saw upon his entrance disturbed him greatly: the monks were lethargic and depressed and their bodies were emaciated; the prolonged mental activity of translation was an imbalance and, as with all imbalances, was beginning to destroy them. Bodidharma explained to them that as the mind and body are inextricably linked, the relationship between them must be continually rejuvenated and rebalanced otherwise disease (dis-ease) would follow. After much meditation, Bodidharma designed a set of exercises to bring about the rejuvenation of the Shaolin monks' body–mind relationship. These exercises formed the basis of what is now Chi Kung and Kung Fu. The Chi Kung exercises presented in this book are scaled-down versions of Bodidhama's original series and have been adapted for modern life.

During his time at the monastery, Bodidharma also wrote several classic texts, introduced the monks to Indian Martial Art and reintroduced the concept of Chi (the ancient art of extracting energy from the air via the breath) into Kung Fu. As time went by, the monks developed a deeper connection with their body movement and so began to understand the natural laws inherent in the human body and its machinations. However, this dynamic connection to their own bodies soon lent itself to meditating on nature itself and the movements contained therein, and hence they began to experience themselves as part of nature. This had a profound effect on the development of Kung Fu, as the monks allowed themselves to be 'taught' by nature directly. For example, by meditating upon animals they came to understand the most natural methods of adapting to their environment and defending themselves against predators; and by meditating upon water they learned how to change the shape of their body in a continuous, 'flowing' manner. We can see both of these examples embodied in the original animal forms (a form is a long series of movements used for practising Kung Fu techniques), which were movements based on the animals (such as the tiger, monkey, snake and white crane) that they were mimicking. As time went on and the monks got stronger, their life dictated that they develop a direct martial application to their movements, as they were being attacked and robbed on their travels to nearby markets.

This direct connection with nature went hand in hand with the spiritual teachings of Taoism, the dominant religion in China between AD 310 and AD 580. The teachings of Taoism were well documented by Confucius (born: 551 BC) and Lao Tzu (born: *circa* 6th century BC), both great philosophers who preached about the evolution of man to such a level that he becomes one with the Tao, again emphasizing the importance of harmonization.

This, I admit, is a condensed history lesson, but it illustrates a few fundamental points about Kung Fu:

1 *Kung Fu was originally a tool to help strengthen the relationship between the mind and the body to make the practitioner stronger in life.*
2 *The first purpose of Kung Fu was to fight disease.*
3 *Kung Fu led to a much deeper understanding of the laws of nature by working through the body.*

Thus, it is important right from the start to understand that the correct study of Martial Art must have both internal (your relationship with yourself) and external (your relationship with the outside world) aspects intact. Like the two halves of the Yin/Yang symbol – separate, yet containing a small representation of the other (a spot) – these aspects must be shown to relate to each other, and helping you to understand this principle is one of the primary aims of this book. When we unlock our understanding of this relationship, we increase the use of (and the number of possibilities for using) our Martial Art training in everyday life. This understanding develops a sense of balance and by using the exercises presented in this book, it is my wish

FIGURE 1

that you develop this sense and become open to the possibilities of how it can accentuate your life. The extraordinary thing about authentic Martial Art is that you work through your own body and build a relationship with it in order to understand about the power of balance through your own experiences. This direct understanding will then begin, quite naturally, to find its way into the other primary areas of your being, namely your mind and your emotions. Then, slowly, a new perception of yourself will begin to emerge where the body, mind and emotions work in dynamic harmony with each other, bringing extensive integration or 'oneness' with yourself and your environment.

The Intelligent Warrior

The title of this book, *The Intelligent Warrior*, was not chosen flippantly. The etymology of the word 'intelligence' comes from two words: 'inter', which means 'between', and 'legere', which means 'to choose'. Thus, the word 'intelligence' implies a sense of balance, an ability to stand between two things and then make a decision, or the intention to take action in one direction or

The Intelligent Warrior

another; indeed, the word 'intends' means 'to stretch out' or 'to move in one direction'. On the other hand, the word 'warrior' means 'bringer of chaos or war' and this, at first sight, might seem to contradict the word 'intelligence'. After all, why would anyone want to bring chaos into his or her life? However, we all have both conscious and unconscious fears that affect our day-to-day decisions and actions, and bring about the same situations in our lives repeatedly. This can make us feel trapped or imprisoned at times in our lives when varying degrees of intensity or stress arise, and in order to free ourselves of these fears we must become *aware* of them in order to 'open' to them or 'throw some light upon them'. We enter a state of chaos when we sense warring factions within ourselves, but only by seeing and accepting this state of chaos can we gradually bring some balance and understanding into our lives.

The Meaning of Kung Fu

The term Kung Fu roughly translated means time spent working on something in direct relationship to yourself so that your skill and yourself simultaneously evolve. Thus, Jimi Hendrix was a Kung Fu guitarist, Claude Monet was a Kung Fu painter and Confucius was a Kung Fu philosopher. A martial artist works on himself through the medium of his or her own body; the *body* is their instrument.

The art of expressing the human body was one of Bruce Lee's favourite topics. He maintained that learning Martial Art should ultimately allow you to express yourself 'honestly' (by this he meant to free of the confines of thought and habits) to be able to adapt to your environment in times of stress. Therefore, Kung Fu really means time spent working on yourself; it is a reinvestment of energy in yourself. We will deal with this principle at great length in this book, for one of the first things that must happen during your training is for you to gain control of your energy so that you do not continually dissipate it with physical, mental or emotional imbalanced states of being that are elicited by fear and its related emotions. And just as a good company reinvests some of its profits back into itself in order to adapt, survive and change in response to the prevailing climate, you as a martial artist must reinvest your energy back into yourself to become stronger and more able to meet the responsibilities that your life demands. You will then be able to defend against imbalance in yourself and recognize the effect that people and external/internal conditions have on you. This is the truth of real self-defence, and any discussion about Martial Art must consider this.

Common Misunderstandings

THE PUBLIC

I have had many conversations with martial artists and the public about Martial Art, and the one thing that strikes me is that everybody thinks they know what it is. Interestingly, it is a subject that seems to provoke people into expressing strong opinions. The top-five reactions of people when I am introduced as a Martial Art instructor are:

1   *'I better stay away from you then' or 'I won't get on your wrong side!' usually said in a jovial tone and followed by a little smile as if they were the first person ever to think of such a quip. It is a tedious reaction because it is immediately assumed that I have a propensity to resort to physical violence, when in fact true*

Martial Art is about harmonization and not the use of inappropriate force to dominate someone.

2 *Holding a bottle of beer or cream cake at a party tends to elicit the response, 'I thought you were supposed to be super fit and weren't supposed to consume things like that!' This reaction expresses the attitude that in order to be a martial artist you must live a life of saintliness and purity, which is rubbish because a martial artist must open up to everything, including 'temptations', in order to adapt. It is not a question of denial but rather a question of experiencing and discarding what is useless, one of the fundamental laws of adaptability.*

3 *The person immediately takes a comic fighting posture, gives the customary war chant 'Hiiiii ya!' and follows up with a reference to the '70s cartoon* Hong Kong Fooey*. Some people deal with their fear of Martial Art by turning it into a caricature.*

4 *They proceed to explain what Martial Art is and tell me how they were once a black belt and that their master could do amazing feats such as walk along walls and defeat multiple attackers with a single touch of his finger. This is indicative of a particularly pernicious attitude bred in people who train in martial sport; it is an overly competitive attitude that is usually based on their own feelings of impotence.*

5 *They immediately adopt an attitude of subservience and over-the-top reverence for my illuminating presence. This type of person tends to want somebody else to take responsibility for them and always looks for answers from the outside instead of from within themselves.*

Why have I gone to the trouble of outlining these somewhat comical responses? Because it is my belief that Martial Art, largely due to the huge media attention lavished upon it, has been grossly misrepresented and misunderstood by the public. Why is this important? Because many people, both men and women, are suffering from a lack of teaching to help them cultivate their warrior spirits truly and fully.

MARTiAL ARTiSTS

The media is not solely to blame for this. So-called martial artists themselves also perpetuate misrepresentations. Three of the most current misrepresentations are:

1 *The Internal School. The main culprits here are people who do T'ai Chi in satin suits and funny slippers in the park on Sunday. They proliferate quasi-Eastern mysticism that preaches about Chi, the importance of yielding and how you can use your energy to redirect your opponent's force and cast aside knife-wielding maniacs with the calmest of demeanours. These people are playing a very dangerous game because a real street encounter with someone who actually wants to do physical harm is a brutal business and your training must reflect this. The internal side is essential in Martial Art but is impotent unless accompanied by the external.*

2 *The External School. People who practise in these types of schools believe that training for martial sport is the same as for Martial Art. One of the greatest crimes that the Western world has committed towards Martial Art is imbuing it with a sense of sport. All over the West, 'martial artists' compete for glittering trophies, glory and adulation in Martial art competitions when in fact scoring points in a tournament has very little to do with either real self-defence or developing the finer sensitivity inherent in artistic training – a mugger is not going to recognize the fact that you have just scored three points for tapping him in*

the ribs. If you only train for scoring points then that is all that will ever emerge when you are in a real situation. Training in this manner also tends to engender arrogant mental and emotional habits that can spill over into your daily lives. This school of training has come about largely because the Western world's first real introduction to Martial Art came via America and so was filtered through their powerful sense of sport. We will deal with this topic in more detail later.

3   **The Street Fighter School.** This is proliferated by people who see themselves as 'hard'. Their attitude is that Martial Art has to be as aggressive as possible because street fights are so bloody and brutal that you can only win if you are 'hard', and think that the best way of training is either for you to beat people up or to get your fellow students to try to beat you up. From one point of view, this is probably the safest of the misrepresentations and the closest to the truth but it is two-dimensional and these people are dangerously missing the point: actual physical confrontation for most people is fairly rare, but conflict exists everywhere. It can also be a very dangerous attitude to take because it increases Yang energy (aggression, anger etc.), which increases the chances of you starting an unnecessary fight and even seriously hurting somebody, consequently increasing the chances of ending up in prison with plenty of time to contemplate what you have lost. I therefore reiterate my point that **physical confrontation for most people is a fairly rare event, but conflict is a natural part of life and is present much of the time**.

The misrepresentations proliferated by the media are too many and varied to go into here, but the most dangerous are the ridiculous types of fight scenes we see in movies today. These lengthy scenes comprise bodies flying, jumping and running along walls, and I am sorry to say that real street fights are never like this. Instead, they tend to be brutal, messy and quite short. It is important to understand that the roots of Martial Art are very far away from the acrobatics and gymnastics portrayed by the entertainment industry. Moreover, you must be clear in your mind what it is you are training for; if you want your Martial Art training to have an effect in your life then you must spend time studying the situations and scenarios that you may encounter.

The Difference between Martial Art and Martial Sport

So, having looked at some of the more common misrepresentations of Martial Art let us now look at what it actually should be. As mentioned previously there is a great difference between Martial Art and martial sport; in fact, most things described as Martial Art are actually martial sport. Martial Art deals with the art of expressing the human body and develops man's innate sense of harmonization, adaptation and exploration. Martial sport, on the other hand, is far more concerned with domination and emphasizes winning as the primary objective; this can have a very detrimental effect on those who practise it as it breeds a very limited two-dimensional perception of the world. It does not teach the human being how to evolve or how to accept Yin and Yang with equal respect or how to accept winning and losing with the same spirit.

Nor does it teach of the presence of the third dimension: balance. The tradition of Martial Art teaches us how to respect our bodies and exercise them in a manner that will preserve them in older age. Martial sport uses the body as a vehicle for glory and utilizes high-impact exercise to get the quickest results possible, and the emphasis is actually from the outside in. The martial sport practitioner seeks material affirmation of their worth as a martial artist, which might include building bigger muscles, acquiring as many trophies as possible, wearing the most elaborate clothing or breaking the most boards. This is a highly dangerous form of training as it tends to build a false image of oneself and bring an overestimation of one's abilities. If correct focus is not taught, the mind will learn to daydream repeatedly about being the star of one's own show, but anyone who has a modicum of experience in street fighting knows how crippling this image of oneself can be. The pure barbarity of real combat wipes out this illusion mercilessly. The most common effect when faced with an actual conflict is that the practitioner will freeze and engage in negative internal conversation about how they should be doing better or what friends are thinking of them. I have seen many skilled martial sport practitioners freeze and be reduced to the most basic form of body mechanics when faced with a drunken, little delinquent who was not afraid of violence.

Another aspect of martial sport, which I personally find astounding, is that so many practitioners end up with serious injuries, which can never really heal. These include destroyed knee ligaments, broken and arthritic hands, various back injuries, detached retinas, fallen arches, and breathing problems caused by broken noses and poor posture. Such injuries usually occur in competitions or regular training that allow full-contact sparring or from trying to attain a material goal such as large muscles or the next coloured belt. By training in this way, the wish to learn how to defend oneself ended up with the practitioner being even less able (due to injury) to defend himself than when he or she first walked in the dojo's (Japanese word for training room) door.

It is also true that training in martial sport tires the body and makes it age quicker. It takes many years to build something of quality and authenticity, and your body is no different. Remember that the term 'Kung Fu' means time spent working, so patience and perseverance need to be cultivated in the practitioner in order to build a quality 'vessel' or body that is integrated and whole.

Key Concepts in Martial Art

An intelligent warrior should begin cultivating the ability to express themselves from the inside out, *not* to seek an image of themselves from the outside in, as if in a mirror. Similarly, they must cultivate an understanding of discipline as a self-imposed set of parameters that helps attain goals, and not as an outside force beating them into shape or a bitter pill that has to be swallowed. The Chinese use the analogy of pruning a tree, for if it is pruned correctly it will bear greater fruit in the spring; so too, if we curb some of our overextended branches (such as putting a stop to engaging in negative emotion or thought) we will gradually develop more internal power. Martial Art should work to develop the body in a holistic manner in accordance with nature, which means evolving the body, mind and spirit harmoniously.

To understand this further we could represent this in a symbolic form, as symbols were originally used to bypass the intellectual functions and represent to the unconscious mind the ideas in

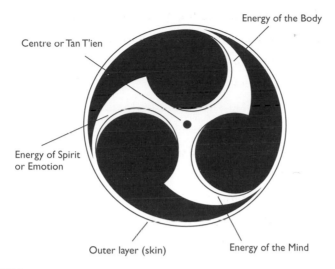

Energy of the Body

Centre or Tan T'ien

Energy of Spirit
or Emotion

Outer layer (skin)

Energy of the Mind

FIGURE 2

question in an energetic format *(see Figure 2).* The dot in the middle
of the symbol represents the centre or Tan T'ien, the point that we
are first trying to stabilize so that everything else can orientate
itself around it. The three circling tadpole-like shapes represent the
primary energies: the body, mind and spirit. These are dynamically
represented for they are continually moving in a cycle of imbalance
and rebalancing. The circle that encompasses the Tan T'ien and the
three energies is the outer level of your body, which includes
your skin, eardrums and eyes. It is at this level that vibrations from
the outside world actually enter your inner world. The energy of
the body deals with our physical nature and encompasses the
physiological, biomechanical and biochemical aspects of your body.
The energy of the mind represents your thought processes and
other functions controlled by the brain. The energy of spirit deals
with the emotions and a gradual refinement of emotional reaction
into feeling. The Chinese character for spirit does not lend itself
to direct interpretation into Western language; however, in the
context of this book I will use the word spirit to represent our

emotional energy rather than in any 'spiritual' context. Having said that, Martial Art should at some point lead us to a spiritual dimension. It is not the scope of this book to deal with this in depth, but it is common sense that our bodies are part of nature and they have been built on the same laws that this planet and universe have been built on. It therefore stands to reason that if we build a connection with our body and bring it more into accordance with the way nature intended then we should begin to resonate with life on a much larger scale. Whether you call it God, The Great Spirit, Allah, Vishnu or the Tao, the awakening to life on a much larger scale is part of the very roots of Kung Fu.

The symbol is also what is known as a paradoxicon in that it stimulates the balance between foreground/background perceptions. When looking at the symbol you may perceive the three aforementioned tadpole-like shapes or you may perceive a three-bladed Shurikan (throwing star). This stimulation of the mechanics of vision is essential in Martial Art training and is a subject we will return to.

Now that we have clarified to some degree what Martial Art is and is not, we can begin to approach the question of authentic self-defence. The following introduces some key concepts that I will refer to at various points throughout the book.

THE HOLISTIC CONCEPT OF SELF-DEFENCE

At the heart of this book lies the practice of holistic self-defence (from the Greek word 'holos' meaning 'whole', and related to the word 'holy'), which is a viewpoint that allows us to look at self-defence from a very wide perspective and one that is in accordance with the laws of nature. The key concept in holistic self-defence is the principle of 'homeostasis', a term used by the medical profession to define the natural healthy state of an organism. The *Merriam-Webster Dictionary* definition for homeostasis is: 'The ability or tendency of an organism or cell to maintain internal equilibrium by adjusting its physiological processes.' We can understand from this definition that a continual process of balance is essential for the maintenance of health. Holistic self-defence looks at the concept of homeostasis not only in the body (as is the focus of Western medicine) but also in the realms of thought and emotion, and it expands to encompass the status quo or 'outer' conditions of our life. Another way of putting this would be that practising holistic self-defence protects you from actual physical attacks, negative thought, negative emotion, viruses, poor posture, addictions and anything that will throw the body out of balance.

We all have an internal balance that allows us to hold together an external balance that could be seen as the status quo or homeostasis of our life. During our daily life we are constantly making decisions, which are followed by actions to maintain our homeostasis. For instance, we plan ahead with money so that we do not end up homeless, we try to see friends and family to fulfil our emotional needs, and so on. This does not mean a homeless person has no balance, it simply means that the homeostasis they maintain in their life is different. However, from time to time something of a much larger magnitude may enter into one's life and throw it completely out of balance requiring some form of 're-action' or rebalancing. Examples include losing a job, the death of a loved one, a partner having an affair, winning the lottery or getting a promotion. Imbalance can occur from both 'positive' and 'negative' events, and sometimes we even need to consciously disrupt the balance of our life in order to move on and grow (for instance, quitting your job to set up your own business). The essential point is that the process of rebalancing through a sense of balance is our primary tool for self-defence, and that our bodies are continually engaged in this process of homeostasis on many different levels; moreover, it is one of the keys to our ability to adapt and survive. In this way, an extremely negative person could be viewed as a virus entering your life, which you may or may not catch a similar illness from, or somebody trying to strike you could be viewed as a disease trying to gain a hold of your body, which you repel and so keep yourself in balance. In *The Science of Homeopathy* George Vithoulkas writes:

> ...every organism possesses a defence mechanism which is constantly coping with stimuli from both internal and external sources. This defence mechanism is responsible for maintaining a state of homeostasis, which is a state of equilibrium between processes tending to disorder the organism and processes that tend to maintain order. Understanding precisely how this defence mechanism works is vital, for any significant impairment of its function rapidly leads to imbalance and finally death.
>
> **Vithoulkas (1986: 16)**

To understand and strengthen this defence mechanism is very much in keeping with the philosophy of Kung Fu (time spent working on yourself). It calls one to practise proactive health, *to strengthen the ground on which influences fall rather than trying to destroy and control influences that we deem threatening.*

The Intelligent Warrior

THE FIGHT-OR-FLIGHT RESPONSE

Throughout the course of this book I will refer to the fight-or-flight response. This response has been evolved over countless centuries and is triggered instinctively by the body (via the autonomic nervous system) when it perceives it is under attack. Some of the reactions that make up the response are as follows:

- *Increased metabolism, heart rate and breathing (to increase energy levels).*
- *Surge in CO_2 production (to prepare for increased intake of O_2).*
- *Release of natural adrenalin, morphine and cortisol into the body (to increase power and control of pain).*
- *Stomach begins to shut down (to make more blood available for the muscles), which tends to cause nausea.*
- *Pupils dilate (to increase visual acuity), which has a tendency to interfere with our visual perception.*
- *Release of coagulants into the bloodstream (to stop bleeding if cut) – prolonged exposure can cause heart attacks in later life.*
- *Blood is pulled away from the skin's surface (to stop excessive bleeding), which may cause leg tremors and cold sweats.*
- *Blood is routed away from the frontal reasoning part of the brain into the more instinctual parts located towards the back of the brain.*

One of the most significant points about this extraordinary instinctual defence mechanism is that it is fired when the body *perceives* it is under attack. This means that even if the threat is not remotely life-threatening (as when we watch a scary movie) the body will still fire the fight-or-flight response to some degree. This is the major cause of what is popularly known as stress and can, over a long period of time, have serious repercussions on our mental, physical and emotional health. The fight-or-flight response was designed for real danger, for sudden spurts of intense life-preserving activity; the body throws itself out of its normal homeostasis in order to protect itself better, and then returns fairly quickly afterwards to its normal state, which it can generally deal with quite well. However, what we see prevalent in today's society is much less intense reactions spread over a longer period of time, and the body cannot cope well with this. The threats that might set the response off in this case might be an abusive boss or partner, money problems, bullying, anxiety about the future, regrets about the past, phobias or low self-esteem. An Intelligent Warrior must become extremely familiar with the fight-or-flight response (the body's most powerful response) because it has a huge effect on our homeostasis.

PROACTiVE HEALTH AND THE CYCLiCAL NATURE OF HEALTH

The correct practice of Martial Art strengthens our 'constitution' by the practice of proactive health and understanding the cyclical nature of health and disease in the body. Western medicine spends a lot of time, money and effort researching and hunting down new microbes, bacteria, viruses, etc., and then developing powerful drugs that kill them. This obsession has blinded them to the fact that it is the constitutional susceptibility of the victims that creates a large proportion of the disease that exists. This blindness leads to the deployment of increasingly toxic drugs, which themselves are becoming a significant public health menace and disturb even further the fine balance that nature has created.

Proactive health means working at the maintenance of your health or homeostasis on a regular basis whilst you are in good health, so as to strengthen your immune and other self-defence systems in the body and therefore lessen your susceptibility to illness. This is a fundamentally different attitude to waiting until we get sick and then going to the doctor and asking them to heal us. Over the last 30 years people have generally become a lot more health conscious and are joining gyms, taking up jogging, modifying their diets or perhaps learning to play a new sport, but although this is a movement in the right direction, a greater depth of understanding is possible through the practice of holistic self-defence where body, mind and spirit are strengthened simultaneously. For instance, your body must always be exercised in relation to the Law of Gravity *(see page 168)*, if you go jogging but are not aware of a misalignment in your spine or foot you will soon cause injury there; if you do not train your mind to focus correctly during exercise you will cultivate a dangerous split between your mind and body caused by daydreaming; and desiring the next material affirmation of your superiority (trophies, belts and so on) or cultivating the emotions of winning over losing will have a severe impact on the evolution of your emotional life.

Understanding the cyclical nature of health and disease is one of the keys to maintaining a steady input of energy into our homeostasis. For example, if a person walks with a slouch, they may not notice any detrimental effects to their health immediately, but because this slouch causes a slight compression of the ribcage, their breathing is always mildly impaired. If this slouch occurs only once it will not be dangerous, but if it occurs over the cycle of years it will cause serious disease in later life. Proactive health uses the same simple understanding to strengthen homeostasis in the body – for example, if by building awareness to your spine you gradually learn the correct positioning for it and then gradually encourage a movement to the correct upright position at times during the day, over the cycle of years you will then defend yourself against ill health brought on by bad posture.

We could equally apply this concept to poor mental and emotional habits – for example, if patterns of negative thought present at a young age are left unchecked, they can cause serious mental-health problems such as depression later in life, but by learning how to focus and quieten the mind at intervals during the day, we can protect our mental health. Equally, excessive feelings of guilt can spread like cancer. Proactively rebalancing our emotional life can protect us from the hoards of doctors trying to shove antidepressants down our throats (for a nice commission).

This simple concept of cyclical health is significant because it means you can work proactively on your health at any time in your day, for example, whilst sitting at your desk or waiting in checkout queues or bus stops, and so on. The Intelligent Warrior in this way makes a decision to become involved in the maintenance of their health at various times of the day. By cultivating this attitude, we begin to bring our Martial Art training directly into our life and so return to the original precepts of Kung Fu.

ACTiON/REACTiON CYCLE

In Meditation (*see page 39*) we use our awareness to practise bringing together the perceptions of our inner and outer worlds, sensing them together as one whole. Our growing sensitivity to this allows us to study the living relationship between our inner and outer worlds. In terms of self-defence, the link between the two is achieved in this order: an event occurs outside ourselves that our senses interpret; the senses turn the impression into an electrical impulse that is transmitted to the brain via the electrical conductors, the nerves; the brain then reacts and we express ourselves in response to the original stimuli. In classic action/reaction fashion, the world reacts in a particular way based upon our reaction, and so the cycle perpetuates. This is the living relationship that continues whether we like it or not. For much of the time it revolves in the background where we do not notice the subtle ways in which we are pulled off balance by various influences, and thus we are unaware of the equally subtle ways that we express our imbalance. Frequently, we carry these reactions around inside us from one environment to another. For instance, when you have a bad day at work you carry it with you home where you continue your negative reactions. The cycle could also just as easily originate from a negative association within oneself, such as suddenly recalling an embarrassing moment, which in turn makes you manifest negativity outwardly. The process of Meditation can build sensitivity to this 'natural' human behaviour, and by so doing can become one of the ways that we consciously participate in the process of homeostasis. By allowing ourselves to approach this idea from an energetic viewpoint, by sensing the energy vibrations coming in via the senses and then sensing the vibrations of our own reaction, we can expand our understanding further. In this way an Intelligent Warrior stands balanced between their inner and outer life in the knowledge that this is the only place where they can truly effect their life. It would be valuable here to return to the previous symbol *(see Figure 3)*

The intersecting arrows represent the three dimensions of the outer world: left to right, forwards and back, up and down. To fully represent this you must imagine the symbol as three-dimensional, with an arrow coming out towards you, so to speak, from the page, or moving into the page. The outer circle is the circle of your awareness where approaching influences are picked up at an early stage.

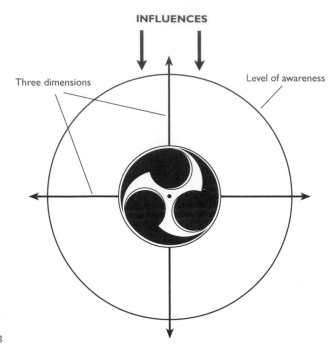

INFLUENCES

Three dimensions

Level of awareness

FIGURE 3

Whenever an influence (which could be an attacker, a virus or a hefty unexpected bill) enters the body it disturbs the body's homeostasis. Sensing that it is being attacked the body will go into its instinctual defence mechanisms, the fight-or-flight response, the strength of which will depend on the intensity of the situation *(see The Principle of Relativity, page 25)*. If the body's centre is weak then severe and prolonged imbalance will occur, which will lead to illness and possibly, indirectly or directly, death. However, if the connection with the body's centre has been developed then it will be strong enough to hold the circling energies of body, mind and spirit in its orbit, allowing a quick and speedy rebalancing or healing to occur.

On a lighter note, an influence could be an inspirational work of art, the focused love of somebody near you, some valuable information gleaned from a book (eh hem!). In such cases, the influence is 'food' for your higher self, which helps you to evolve a finer sense of balance and therefore increase the homeostasis between your body, mind and spirit.

HiGHER HEALTH

The concept of higher health was expressed quite clearly in Chinese medicine and is where the healing process is not only seen as restoring balance after illness but also as a means of evolving the individual into a higher state of 'being'. Moreover, the energy we use to continually heal ourselves from all kinds of disease is not available for this higher purpose. However, participation in the action/reaction cycle allows us to make different choices at critical decision points and so cultivates the Intelligent Warrior within.

THE PRiNCiPLE OF RELATiViTY

When your body receives an impression of an attack, it will instantaneously react with the fight-or-flight response and, depending on the nature of the impression, will react with different levels of intensity. Generally speaking, the more extreme the attack the greater the reaction. So when dealing with the concept of self-defence we must understand the scale that these reactions can fall into. The attack does not necessarily have to be a physical attack against you; it could be something on a smaller scale such as verbal abuse or negative thought. As you can see from Figure 4, at one end of the scale there are life-threatening attacks, including attacks with weapons or by multiple opponents. At the other end of the scale are the ways in which we attack ourselves, including negative and depressive thoughts. Initially it may not be clear why we need to

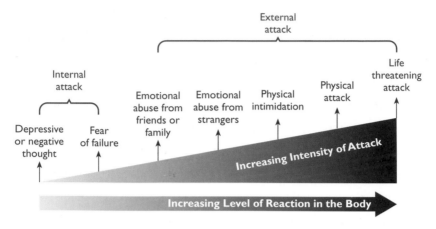

FIGURE 4

study such a wide scale but, as you will see later, we respond to many of life's minor conflicts with our instinctual fight-or-flight response and we can gain valuable insights and experience of ourselves in such situations, which will help immeasurably to deal with more intense reactions.

PRiNCiPLE OF RESONATiON

The Principle of Resonation is one of the governing principles of vibration that I will refer to frequently throughout the book.

The principles of sound dictate that the vibration of any object is communicated through the atmosphere in waves. Each note of the musical scale vibrates at its own frequency, thus each sound wave is shaped uniquely according to its pitch. When two objects with similar pitches are in close proximity to each other, such as two guitars, the vibration purposely caused on one – say, the plucking of the B-string – will cause the B-string on the second guitar to also vibrate (with less intensity) because it resonates at a similar level. This principle is also known as sympathetic vibration and it relates to holistic self-defence in two basic ways:

1   *Being in close proximity to someone who is in an emotionally agitated state will tend to make you resonate a similar state (this is similar to when someone has an 'infectious' laugh).*

2   *If you develop a certain quality or skill in the body (such as a sense of balance) it will tend to resonate a similar quality in the mind and emotions. The* Chambers Dictionary *(1994) uses this example in its definition of the word 'resonance':* The complex of bodily responses to an emotional state, or of emotional responses to a situation.

INTERNAL CONVERSATION

Internal conversation is a subject broached by almost every system of Meditation that I have studied. Awareness of the continual conversation that churns inside our heads and the gradual conviction of its totally habitual nature is one of the first goals of Meditation. Internal conversation has a tendency towards negativity and being judgmental. Gaining a certain degree of freedom from internal conversation is essential for the Intelligent Warrior for it prevents us from receiving the impressions from the outside world directly. For example, something someone says triggers an association in your mind and you immediately start engaging in an internal conversation about it. This means that you are not only taking in the impression of the person talking directly but also listening to your own conversation, which is likely to lead you to lose track of what they are saying.

Internal conversation is also sometimes known as associative thinking because it uses associations to self-perpetuate. For instance, you are reading these words when suddenly your stomach grumbles, you tell yourself you are hungry and deserve a break, you start to think about what you are going to eat, perhaps imagine going to your favourite sandwich shop and recall bumping into an old friend the last time you were there, recall some of the things you used to do when you were younger, think 'What a long time ago that was, is it really 10 years?', 'What have I done with that time? I should have taken that other job...' and so on. At the same time, you sat in exactly the same place trying to read. If left unchecked this associating will go on relentlessly from the moment we wake up to the moment we fall asleep and rob us of many experiences and opportunities available in the present moment.

Internal conversation walks hand in hand with daydreaming and provides a running dialogue to the pictures thrown up by your mind. As mentioned previously, there is a tendency for this habitual talking to turn negative so our daydreams can end up with a picture of ourselves begging on the streets or something equally catastrophic! The Intelligent Warrior must learn to protect himself or herself against internal conversation because it burns a tremendous amount of energy, destroys self-esteem and has a tendency to increase in intensity when in a stressful situation.

ATTACHMENT, DETACHMENT AND NONATTACHMENT

The concept of attachment, detachment and nonattachment comes directly from Taoism and is basically another expression of balance in that attachment can be seen as the Yang principle, detachment as the Yin principle and nonattachment as the balancing force between them. When a conflict or powerful event occurs in our life it makes us react. Our reaction then tends to polarize into either Yang (attachment), where we become obsessed by the occurrence, cannot stop talking or thinking about it and may even take some rash action on account of this, such as accusing someone of something before we have all the facts. The opposite reaction, Yin (detachment), is where we try to deny that the event ever occurred and pretend that the problem does not exist – for example, many people get into serious financial difficulties because they are afraid to face up to mounting debts. What these two reactions have in common is that they burn a lot of energy and stop you from seeing the event in an objective light, in turn stopping you from taking the appropriate action, which always involves an *intelligent* decision. Nonattachment allows you to sense these Yin and Yang perspectives simultaneously for in reality an Intelligent Warrior needs them both. The Yang reaction teaches us not to be blasé about events; it is the power by which we take action on something and gives us the strength to 'grab the bull by the horns'. However, without the sensitivity from the Yin perspective, which teaches us to hold back perhaps to gather more information or to read the situation fully, we will be in danger of becoming a 'bull in a China shop' and making a particular situation a lot worse than it was to start out with.

The way to practise nonattachment is always to move into the present moment, for it is only here that you can pull your energy away from the imbalanced reaction. This is one of the skills developed in the practice of Meditation. By doing this we learn to become more sensitive to the Yin and Yang reactions within ourselves so that eventually any small fluctuation is sensed. A good working example would be when an experienced poker player makes himself or herself very quiet inside and enters into the present moment in order to read the tiny reactions (called 'poker tells') given off by the other players that give away their bluffs or inability to conceal excitement over the cards they are holding. This allows the Intelligent Warrior to know 'when to hold them and when to fold them' as the country singer Kenny Rogers would say!

Another helpful way of visualizing this essential concept is to look at Figure 5. Here we see our Yin and Yang reactions represented in a waveform, which tends to be how emotional reactions operate – we go up but at some point there is a corresponding low. Moreover, each situation will make you react in a slightly different way (for instance, even the most aggressive bouncer may try to avoid a confrontation with his wife when drunkenly stumbling in late after work!).

The key to nonattachment is firstly to ensure that when you are up (Yang) and taking direct action on something you remain aware of the Yin principle. For instance, be sensitive to the effect you are having on the situation. Secondly, make sure that when you are down (Yin) you to try to find the Yang energy. For instance, the classic Yin reaction is depression and, as any experienced therapist

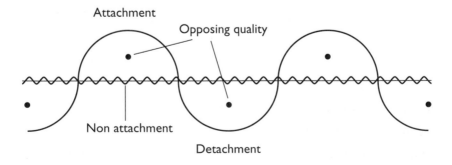

FIGURE 5

will tell you, the key to relieving depression is to take action. So, instead of getting depressed about money problems, for example, face them and take action to rectify the situation.

Nonattachment does not mean that you suppress your reactions — reactions are part of what is to be human and are necessary for life — but it does mean that you become more sensitive to them in order to sense earlier when you are being pulled off balance. This is represented by the smaller waveform that is close to the straight line (the point of balance) and is a much finer level of vibration or sensitivity. In this way, you learn not to commit so much energy to your reactions, which will in turn allow you to pay more attention to your goals.

PREPARATION FOR THE UNEXPECTED

As mentioned earlier, we must always keep in mind what it is that Martial Art is training us for. The aim of this book is to gain an insight into how Martial Art strategies and practices can help you in everyday situations. Therefore, we must learn how to prepare for this eventuality. One of the main differences between martial sport and Martial Art is the fact that in a sport situation you know where, you know when, you know how (what rules) and you know whom you are going to fight. A real situation, on the other hand, very often means that you do not know any of these things. Martial Art should teach you to be prepared for the unexpected and then to be able to adapt almost instantaneously to this unknown force. I once witnessed a cyclist riding down the road in a busy city centre, quite obviously daydreaming about being somewhere else. As the cyclist rode down the road, a careless van driver (who was about 10 metres away) opened his door and the cyclist continued towards it, saw it just in time, then reacted instinctively by swerving. The cyclist missed the door but his overreaction meant that he lost his balance and came crashing heavily to the ground.

This story illustrates very well what a real conflict situation is like. The cyclist was daydreaming and not living in the present moment. This state of 'waking sleep' tends to be extremely common in the average human being and because of it, the cyclist was not aware of the door opening soon enough to recognize it and make a controlled evasive manoeuvre. Instead, it was left to the cyclist's reflexes, operating at a much finer level of recognition, to perform the manoeuvre. However, he oversteered due to his body's reaction to fear and consequently his balance was destroyed and no further riding technique was possible. The situation happened totally out of the blue — one minute the cyclist was daydreaming of holiday beaches or winning the lottery and the next minute the cruel reality of life almost literally slapped him in the face. His inner state changed with lightning speed from one of habitual daydreaming to one of extreme fear. In that split second his whole life and state of being had changed, perhaps not for ever but certainly for the near future. This is exactly what happens in any unexpected situation.

So, we must first build a robust state of awareness so that opening doors, depressive thoughts, abusive parents or bosses, or physical attacks do not surprise us and we become aware of their presence at the earliest opportunity. We must then build a presence that is strong enough to deal with the situation, as opposed to an absence (a symptom of which is the aforementioned daydreaming). Then and only then will we be able to rely on any technique that we may have learned to deal with the attack.

THE FOUR MAiN AREAS OF STUDY

Having studied Martial Art now for over 25 years, it has become clear to me that there are four main areas of study that need to be addressed. These areas make up as it were the anatomy of a martial artist. They are each linked and interdependent on one another, and provide a different perspective of the same picture. A practical understanding of each area is essential if one is hoping to study Martial Art authentically. The four main studies are:

1 **Meditation:** *This is really about the relationship you have with yourself and it opens the lines of communication between your mind and your body via sensation. This develops a state of awareness sensitive to both the inner (Yin) and outer (Yang) aspects of your life and strengthens the balance between your body, mind and spirit; I will refer to this balance as your presence. Awareness and presence form your first and second lines of defence respectively.*

2 **Chi Kung:** *The practice of Chi Kung harmonizes breath and movement. It is, if you like, a moving form of Meditation. It develops internal energy, strengthens the natural breath processes and develops freedom of movement. Chi Kung enables you to meditate whilst moving.*

3 **Martial Science:** *This is the study of body mechanics and the laws that govern human aggression. It is the study of techniques and their applications. It introduces various strategies based on common patterns of attack. By studying Martial Science, you will learn how to meditate whilst in relation to another human being.*

4 **Martial Art:** *Martial Art trains your ability to express yourself in all kinds of conflict situations. This is the culmination of the previous areas of study. It allows you to find areas in your life where you can apply your self-defence skills. Martial Art enables*

you to meditate whilst dealing with real situations in your life (as opposed to the artificial setting of a dojo or gym).

HOW TO APPROACH THiS BOOK

This book should be used as a working manual that can be dipped into on a daily basis, acting as a reminder and general guide to those of you who are searching for the martial way. It is also a good idea to read it from cover to cover to get an overall picture of what the study of Martial Art should include.

I am using this book to present Martial Art to you as a tool and, like all tools, it will only be meaningful to you when you use it practically in your life. This does not require you to go out and start conflicts in order to fulfil your training. In fact, the truth of conflict and its associated fears is that it is a part of everyday life that we are continually affected by – we are often attacked from within by our own negative thoughts and attitudes towards ourselves; conflicts arise between people who love each other; fear exists between people who work together; people, whether consciously or unconsciously, send negative thoughts or 'vibes'; and there is always a possibility of physical intimidation which, while relatively rare in most people's lives, is increasing in all our lives all the time. If you embrace the fact that attack in some form is integral to our lives, then you will start to see our training from a much wider perspective. By the time you have finished reading this book you should have gained an understanding of the nature and effects of fear in your life. Moreover, you will have a good understanding of the strategies that could be employed to overcome the debilitating effects of fear and aggression.

If I appear to repeat myself during the course of this book, it is because some points need to be reiterated before their significance can be realized. The process of conscious repetition is essential to Martial Art, for it is only by repeating carefully (practising) a particular move or aspect, that your body, mind and spirit can begin to embody the underlying principles. It is because of this that delving deeply into the spiritual ramifications of this kind of work is beyond the scope of this book. It can take you to that door, but it will not open it very far. This is primarily because a very thorough grounding in the physical and practical aspects is needed before we can truly experience the spiritual benefits of Martial Art.

You are reading these words now for a reason; perhaps this book caught your eye on a bookshop's shelf, perhaps somebody gave it to you because they felt that it could help you with particular situations that you are experiencing. Whatever the reason, it is important that before you start grappling with the ideas and concepts in this book, you are clear, as much as possible, why you are interested in the martial path and what you wish to gain from studying it. The true martial path is not a particularly easy one since it will ask you to face things in yourself that you would perhaps wish to keep in the dark, and it demands that you slowly bring your ego into perspective and allow a more 'human' being to take control of your life. This process requires you to be open to the relationship that exists in you with the things that part of you would most like to avoid, namely areas where pain and fear operate. Because of this fact, there will be times when you meet great resistance in yourself to forging ahead and keeping the process going. Remember that you are investing your energy and attention back into yourself and by so doing strengthening yourself at the very core of your being, thereby becoming more effective, stronger and able to meet all that life demands of you. This is the real meaning and purpose of Kung Fu: to provide a tool that you can use to deal with your daily battles, whether they be against violent attacks of a criminal nature, abusive bosses, partners, strangers, or negative thoughts and attitudes within you, or perhaps just to fight for what you want out of life and to deal with the many failures it takes to make a success. Nothing that is worth anything in life comes cheaply or easily. Conflict is an inescapable part of life and always carries with it a good helping of fear and pain; it arises in our life in many different places, some suspected, some unsuspected, and awareness of the possibility of conflict is your first line of defence. If we can keep our original motivations and wishes alive, we can return to the source of our enquiry into Martial Art and strengthen once again our wish to evolve by facing our fears.

AN ENERGETiC LANGUAGE

An Intelligent Warrior needs to develop an energetic language, a communication with his/her own body that allows them to experience their study from the perspectives of the body, mind and spirit. It is only by working from this perspective that we can make the written word come alive, and the process of embodiment can take place. Over time, Westerners have become increasingly more divorced from their own bodies; they view it from the outside, looking back at themselves as if in a mirror and asking questions such as: 'Am I desirable?' 'Are they better than me?' 'Are they better looking than I am?' This is a symptom of a materially based society, and in such a society, it is inevitable that we start to see our own bodies as material objects and begin to have attitudes towards them. This in turn brings feelings of isolation, of separation from ourselves and the world around us; we are wary of people, suspicious of ulterior motives, anxious about the future or afraid of being alone. In this way we become strangers to ourselves, always commenting and judging with our internal conversation and becoming increasingly vulnerable to one of the most powerful fears in man: the fear of not being loved. We have lost the ability to sense our bodies from the inside, to connect, appreciate and celebrate the feeling of life itself within us. Therefore, perhaps the greatest benefit of studying Martial Art is to regain the ability to connect with one's own life and the energies that animate it.

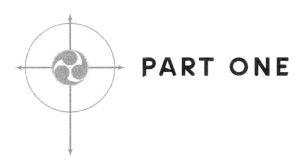

PART ONE

MEDITATION

In terms of meaning, consciousness (mind), energy, and the body are clearly defined as three facets or cooperating functions within one indivisible system. Among these, mind is the initiator of systematic movement, so it is the directorate, or high command. Energy is the capacity of systematic movement. The body is the army.
Ming and Weijia (1994: 11)

Before your opponent can strike you they must first rummage around to find an available hand to do so.   **Sun Li**

introduction

The word 'Meditation' conjures up many different images in people's minds, from shaven-headed Buddhist monks to stoned hippies to New Age dilettantes. Therefore, before beginning our study of Meditation we must clearly define what it is. The word 'Medi-tation' originates from the same root as the words 'medi-ate', 'medi-um', 'medi-an' and, most interestingly, 'medi-cine'. This is significant, not as an etymological exercise, but as a clue as to why the word was first used to describe the practice. We find signposts pointing towards a sense of balance (mediate) and of being in the middle (medium, median), and a hint that somehow this has a part to play in healing (medicine). So, what exactly are we 'mediating' between when we engage in the practice of Meditation? Moreover, what part does it play in Martial Art?

In the practice of Meditation, we are trying, via our attention, to facilitate a connection between the mind and body, which is the foundation that holistic self-defence is built upon. It has been said, in various ways and in many different traditions and teachings, that humans have two bodies: the physical body and, for want of a better phrase, 'the body of attention'. Our physical bodies are rooted in the present moment and, as the laws of time and space govern them, cannot be anywhere else. However, the body of attention is not rooted in the present moment but has the ability to project itself into the past, the future (through use of the memory or imagination) or to a different place (than the physical body). This is commonly known as daydreaming and occurs frequently, for example, how many times have you found yourself turning the page in the book that you are reading to find that, while your eyes read the words, your mind was elsewhere and did not register them? Your physical body had not moved but had remained sitting, continuing the task it had been given (reading), but your body of attention had disappeared to another place in time. The work of the meditative process is to bring the body of attention back into the physical body and to strengthen their connection so that they are less likely to separate so easily. It is only when the physical body and the body of attention are together that we can truly enter into the present moment and receive the many and varied impressions, both from inside and outside, available to us. I cannot emphasize enough the profoundness of this connection and its importance in applying Martial Art to life.

The type of Meditation that is presented here is what I would call Dynamic Meditation and has been specifically developed for the purpose of holistic self-defence. Unlike most usual forms of Meditation, which are done in a sitting or lying position, Dynamic Meditation is done supporting your own weight in a standing position. It is broken down into two complementary halves: Inner and Outer Meditation. Inner Meditation deals with the connection to various aspects of our physicality via our attention – each aspect brings a particular quality or skill to self-defence techniques. Outer Meditation develops the devices we use to receive impressions from the outside world: the senses. Before bringing the two halves together to form one whole awareness, they should first be studied and developed separately, but together they form the basis for the first two lines of defence: awareness and presence.

1 **Awareness** is the first line of defence. If we are not aware that something is attacking us then we cannot apply any intelligence to protect ourselves from it. Awareness is twofold – we have awareness of the physical world around us, but also an awareness of what is going on inside ourselves, such as muscular tension, emotional agitation or internal conversation. By meditating we are bringing the inner and outer aspects together into what the American Indians sometimes describe as a 'seamless web of awareness'. This web functions as an early warning system so that we are not surprised by an attack; it is like radar, or a scout listening to the ground for the sound of approaching hooves. A certain degree of awareness will always be present in the body – many of our instinctive defence mechanisms are triggered by an almost unconscious awareness but this unconscious awareness only goes so far. In terms of what we are trying to study in this book, we wish to understand the mechanics of awareness and to develop this potential.

2 **Presence** is really the aforementioned balance between the body, mind and spirit, for when these aspects of our being come into harmony and we are 'present', a tangible force emanates. Presence starts with the ability to hold some degree of attention in your body, not daydreaming or engaging in internal conversations but feeling your body at this moment in time. This is suggested in the very word 'presence': to be 'present', or 'pre-sense' (what comes before the senses). Thus, without attention in the body, in other words if the attention is not connected to the senses, you cannot 'open' to the present moment, which is the only place that the relationship between your body, mind and spirit can be forged and maintained.

Through the process of Meditation we aim to strengthen this heightened state of awareness and presence. We aim to bring the body, mind and spirit into a state of integration to act as a safeguard, because when we feel fearful, anxious or stressed the relationship between the body, mind and spirit has a tendency to disintegrate. An example of this occurred when I was younger and living in Oxford, England. One day I was sitting on a bus when it stopped outside Queen's College and a then quite famous mathematician boarded. In those days it was imperative to have ready the exact price of the bus ticket, but the professor fumbled in his pocket for the change and took a little longer then the driver would have liked, and was informed of this in no uncertain terms. Immediately, the professor became visibly agitated, mumbling half apologies, turning bright red and sweating. He peered intensely into the hand that held his change and finally handed over the money to the bus driver. However, he had counted the money incorrectly, which further irritated the driver who, cursing, grabbed our poor professor's hand and counted the money out. Here was a bus driver counting for an Oxford professor of mathematics! The impression of this exchange struck me greatly and seemed to really illustrate the debilitating effects that fear can have on us. The poor professor became so disintegrated that he could not even perform the most basic of mathematical calculations. When he was verbally attacked by the bus driver he went into a mild state of shock that disturbed the balance between his body, mind and spirit and rendered his formidable intellect useless.

We all have a certain balance between these three primary energies in the body but, for the most part, the balance is very fragile and we know little to nothing about how it operates. Everyone has one of these areas that is more active than the others, some people are considered intellectual, others more emotional, while still others are more physical. If you have not already started to do so, think about some of the people in your life, including yourself, and you will begin to see what I mean. It is possible through the process of Meditation to become aware of how these forces behave within you and to participate in the process of balancing them. This is one of the reasons why in traditional Kung Fu training, emphasis was placed not only on the fighting skills but also on skills such as calligraphy, music and healing, each demanding a slightly different emphasis on the body, mind and spirit. Whenever we are attacked in any way there is a tendency for the relationship between the body, mind and spirit to disconnect; sometimes we can manage to 'pull ourselves together', but at other times we cannot and we 'go to pieces', 'fall apart', 'come unstuck' or 'lose our head'. If through the regular practice of Meditation we can develop a movement towards integration, strengthening our attention in the body, then we will have a very useful tool that we can call upon when we need it in our lives. The point is that we can strengthen this relationship between the body, mind and spirit just as we would a muscle and by so doing we add a very real and tangible weapon to our arsenal. Therefore, I am not presenting Meditation as a vague notion or practice, but as a practical study. For this to occur you must first gain some understanding of the internal aspect of Meditation.

the basic stance

Before beginning the practice of Meditation it is important to define the physical stance that you are going to adopt in order to meditate. The Chinese call this stance the 'Mar Bou' or 'horse-riding stance', and a variation of it exists in every martial art that I have ever studied. As my Martial Art studies continued, I realized that there was only one correct way for this stance to be taken in order to locate the body's centre of gravity at the Tan T'ien, channel gravity correctly through the skeleton and finely tune the physiological balancing mechanisms in the body. When Bodidharma (*see page 3*) originally instructed the monks in this stance he was quite specific: the feet should be parallel, the fists held upwards at the level of the waist, the knees slightly bent and the weight evenly distributed. In the original Kung Fu schools it was not uncommon for a new student to practice nothing but the Basic Stance for a year or longer, such was the importance that was placed upon it. It is the most balanced posture that a human being can stand in and by taking this physical posture you begin to affect your balance, which through the Principle of Resonation (*see page 26*) affects other areas of your functioning such as your mind and emotions. What follows is a description of this stance starting from the feet and working upwards to the top of the head. I will go into various aspects of 'Mar Bou' in more detail as you progress through the Meditation exercises, but for now follow the description whilst referring to Photographs 1 and 2.

1

2

1 *Stand with your feet slightly wider than shoulder width apart to provide a wider base and therefore more stability to your upright structure (see Align the Body, page 61). The wider you put your feet the more leverage you can get from the ground, but you lose mobility; the closer your feet are together the more mobility you can get, but you lose leverage.*

2 *Make sure that your feet are parallel to each other. This is crucial for correct alignment of the body – having your feet parallel is the natural placement for them, which means that the ligaments in the feet and the knees will be strengthened and balanced correctly in accordance with gravity (see The Art of Walking, page 68).*

3   Bend slightly at the knees. Bending at the knees lowers the centre of gravity in the body, locating it to the Tan T'ien. Bending the knees works closely with the width of your stance to give you balance between power (from the ground) and mobility. The bend in the knees should allow you to drop your centre by approximately 6 inches, which is the optimum place for the centre of gravity to be located and also makes the body feel more grounded, which affects the mind and the emotions.

4   Make sure your spine is straight. A straight spine is the most essential ingredient in maintaining our biomechanical health. It also allows us to judge distance accurately (an indispensable self-defence skill).

5   Make sure you are not leaning forwards as in Photograph 3, or backwards as in Photograph 4.

6   Adjust the angle of your head by tucking your chin in slightly; try to feel that there is a string pulling you up from the top of your head.

7   Hold your hands in a loose fist at about the same level as the navel, gently touching the sides of the body. Tuck your thumbs outside the fist. The hands and arms are not essential for maintaining uprightness but we need to give them an exact form and place when meditating.

Take your time to learn the Basic Stance correctly. It might seem a bit boring but its effects on your health and your ability to practice holistic self-defence are far-reaching. It is this physical stance that forms the root of all other physical positions and techniques; also, by giving a precise form to our physicality we take a great step in bringing form to our thoughts and emotions.

3

4

inner meditation

CENTRiNG THE BODY

> Balance is the all-important factor in a fighter's attitude or stance. Without balance at all times, he can never be effective. **Bruce Lee (1975)**

Centring the body involves connecting the mind to the physical centre of gravity of the body (the Tan T'ien). This centre is approximately one and a half inches below the navel, in the centre of the pelvis. It is the place that you were first nourished from via the umbilical cord and is at the level of the sacrum, which is the first bone made in the body. Both Eastern and Western medicine define the physical centre at this point, and to build a connection with your centre is to communicate with the very core and origins of your being. From a self-defence point of view, having a strong connection with the centre increases your balance and power and reduces the risk of falling.

To start with, this connection (referring back to the quotation at the beginning of this chapter) is made by our 'intention' from the mind

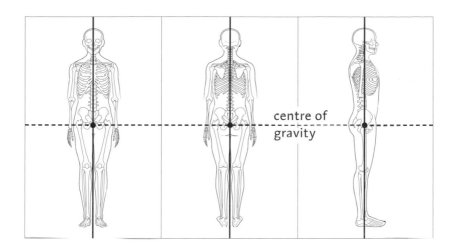

FIGURE 6

(initiator) sending our 'attention' (capacity) to the area of the body (army) that is its centre. From there we begin to 'play' with the two primary mechanisms that allow us to have a sense of where the centre is exactly: pressure sensitivity in the legs and the balancing mechanisms in the inner ear. The placement of the centre is defined in three dimensions: left and right, forwards and back, up and down. By working with these three dimensions we can pinpoint an exact place inside the body that is the centre. These directions correspond to the three semicircular canals in the inner ear, which are filled with fluid and aligned to these dimensions.

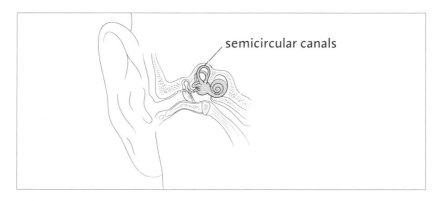

FIGURE 7

1 **Left to Right** *If you look at the exercise to centre the body (page 56), you will see that the first movement oscillates between the left and right leg; this stimulates the pressure sensitivity in both legs. Pressure sensitivity in the legs is one of the main ways that we remain upright; the brain constantly uses the information from each leg to balance itself (it does this by sensing the amount of muscle tension present in each leg). If you think about walking, the pressure is passed from one foot to the other, and as you make your stride the pressure is balanced on each side to form an equal gait. If you have ever injured your foot you will have been reminded of this pressure moving from one side to the other – the moment you stand upright your body uses the pressure in the two legs to maintain its balance. As a martial artist you must develop sensitivity to this so that you become increasingly skilled at keeping a balance between the two legs.*

2 **Forwards and Back** *The next movement oscillates forwards and back (standing in the Basic Stance leaning forwards and leaning back), which stimulates the inner ear, one of the most extraordinary pieces of engineering in the body. As we lean forwards and back the fluid in the inner ear acts much like a builder's spirit level, providing vital information as to whether the head is level or not. The brain stem and the cerebellum (two of the areas of the brain that control reflex movement) are continually monitoring this information from the ear. If we lean too far forwards or back, the brain immediately makes us shift our feet and hands to 'catch' our balance. By evolving our sensitivity to this inner movement of energy, we protect the centre from being lost; if we lose the centre then very soon we will fall over and have to fight or defend ourselves from the ground, which is probably the worst place you can be.*

3 **Up and Down** *The last dimension is up and down (the vertical axis), arguably the most significant of them all as not only is it the*

most common way that we lose our centre but also the connection to this area helps to work against the body's most powerful symptom of the fight-or-flight response: energy travelling upwards. You will see in the exercise on centring the body that the vertical axis is found by relaxing and 'sitting' (similar to sitting down on a chair) into the Basic Stance, so it is a movement of relaxing where you instruct the muscles not necessary for standing to turn 'off'. This is of tremendous significance because in any conflict situation our inner energy travels up and backwards simultaneously turning the muscles 'on' (tension). This type of reaction is the root of many popular sayings such as 'to blow one's lid', or 'to lose one's head'. Becoming in touch with the absolute truth of this statement is one of the keys to self-defence.

In any conflict situation (and we have gone to some length to describe what we mean by conflict) the first movement of self-defence must always be a relaxation and dropping towards the centre. This is not as easy as it would first appear because the aforementioned effect of fear in the body is of always moving the energy up and turning the muscles on. Therefore, by working with the exercise of centring, the body creates a deeper connection or movement towards the centre, and once we have found our centre everything else can orientate itself around it. The stronger the connection with the centre, the more of an anchor we have against this movement upwards of fear in the body.

PHYSICAL IMBALANCE

When we become physically imbalanced we lose our centre in a combination of the above dimensions (left, right, up, down, etc.). If you recall a time when you tripped and fell forwards, or jerked your head back away from something coming towards your head, you will already have a very real impression of physical imbalance. The Basic Stance is the most balanced position a human body can take, and relaxation is fundamental in order to adopt it correctly. When we relax, the body accepts the force of gravity through it *(see Align the Body, page 61)* and naturally begins to find its point of balance. We have evolved by nature an upright spine, so by relaxing and entering into this most balanced of postures we once again move closer to a natural state of being. That does not mean that we have to always walk around with a lowered centre of gravity, but in terms of applying self-defence techniques, the lowered centre is essential. When standing or moving generally in life we can still have this movement of relaxation and dropping down by connecting to our sense of the centre even if our legs are not bent and we are fully upright.

MENTAL IMBALANCE

Working with the physicality of the body is very tangible and we can feel it if we are in the present moment; by the Principle of Resonance *(see page 26)* this sense of balance then begins to teach the other areas of our being: the mind and emotions. Therefore, we begin to feel when our minds become imbalanced; the classic symptoms of this imbalance are a heightened internal conversation and projection into the future or the past with daydreams. For most of us this imbalance goes on all the time inside our heads, but when humans for one reason or another become chronically imbalanced we see this internal conversation starting to manifest itself *outside* ourselves. When this happens people talk aloud to themselves and actually begin to see their daydreams in the form of delusions and hallucinations. In this situation the internal imaginings take over control of the physical body and start to change its position correspondingly; this process happens in much more subtle ways with regular daydreaming. The balancing point for the mind is the present moment, which is the fulcrum between the past and future. To maintain this balance you as an Intelligent Warrior must develop the ability to quieten internal conversation and refrain from daydreaming.

EMOTIONAL IMBALANCE

Emotional imbalance always has a positive or negative charge so we either become overexcited, silly or 'over the top' or we indulge in negative emotions such as anger, self-pity, depression or self-loathing. Emotion is the quickest and most powerful energy in the body and for this reason it is the most 'expensive'. If we become extremely enraged at something, it can take days for the body to rebalance itself. Recall a time when you became extremely emotional about something and remember how the emotional energy took over your physical body, perhaps contorting it into various positions, and how any rational thought was severely impaired. When we find the balancing point for emotions, which is always a sense of stillness, then we can begin to develop or evolve the emotions into feelings and allow them to take a more subtle form such as the composition of a piece of music, poetry or painting or the selection and execution of an appropriate self-defence technique.

THE THREE-DiMENSiONAL POiNT OF BALANCE

The process of searching for balance can be well illustrated by the movement of a pendulum. To start with the pendulum swings in quite large movements from side to side and then gradually, as the force of gravity takes over, the movement decreases until it finds the point of balance (pointing straight down) and it comes to rest. This point of rest is a defining characteristic of your balance but it is not a complete point of rest or stagnation as it is always oscillating in tiny movements between the three dimensions. Think about a tightrope walker making very fine adjustments to stay on the tightrope or a child learning to ride a bike, wobbling from one side to the other until he or she finds a point of balance and stability. In humans the point of balance has many different expressions but the three primary characteristics are relaxation in the body, quietness in the mind and stillness in the emotions. The gradual development of balance through Meditation brings these characteristics to the surface and each can only truly be found in the present moment.

THE EXERCiSE OF CENTRiNG

Centring the body is an essential skill for the Intelligent Warrior for it allows you to hold two opposing forces in your awareness and find a balancing point between them. This is critical for applying intelligence to emotionally charged situations.

Left to Right

This exercise opens awareness to pressure sensitivity in the legs, a device the brain uses continuously to keep us upright, especially when walking.

5   6

1   Stand in the Basic Stance (see page 46) *and close your eyes.*

2   Direct your intention down towards the area of the Tan T'ien
    (an inch and a half below the navel).

3   Slowly shift your weight from the left leg to the right in quite
    large motions, leaning quite far out over each leg (see
    Photograph 5).

4   Relax and be open to the impressions of the pressure as it
    increases in each leg as you move over it.

5   Gradually begin to decrease the movements. Perhaps think of the
    pendulum swinging from side to side as it begins to move to a
    point of rest.

6   Continue until you are only making very small movements but
    can still feel the pressure changing in the legs.

7   Finally, try to come to rest at the exact balancing point between
    the two legs.

Forwards and Back

This movement primarily stimulates the balance-sensing mechanism of the inner ear.

1   *Slowly begin to rock forwards* (see Photograph 7) *and back* (see Photograph 8) *on your feet and feel your weight travelling from the heel to the ball the foot. Try to be sensitive to the place where if you went further you would begin to fall and would have to move your foot to catch your balance.*

7

8

2   *Without losing the sensation of the Tan T'ien, direct your attention to the area of the inner ear.*

3   *Repeat the process in the previous Right to Left exercise, gradually decreasing the movements until you find the balancing point.*

The Intelligent Warrior

Up and Down

1 Open to the sensation of relaxing and sitting into the Basic Stance, as if sitting down on a chair.

2 Push up slightly from the stance and then sit down again into it.

3 Repeat this process, focusing on the sensation of the muscles that are necessary to push you up as opposed to the ones that are used for you to 'sit' into the stance.

4 Try very gently to keep renewing this movement of relaxation (letting go) as you sit down in the stance.

By making large movements to small ones our brain receives, via the pressure sensitivity in the legs and the balancing mechanisms in the inner ear, a wide range of movement from which it can compare the complementary opposites inherent in each section. By working in this way we gradually increase our sensitivity to the interplay between the opposites and become very sensitive to even the slightest movement away from the point of rest in any of the dimensions. This sensitivity means that we are *aware* sooner that our centre is becoming unstable and then, by the process of attention or *presence* in the body, we can correct it accurately with less chance of over-balancing in the opposite direction.

The up-and-down movement of relaxation may take a little while to get the hang of but by relaxing just enough you will become sensitive to the sensation of your weight locating down to the Tan T'ien. This movement of relaxation needs to be accompanied by a command to the muscles to 'let go'. Remember, when you become nervous, stressed or afraid the body has a tendency to turn the muscles 'on', in other words tension creeps into the body; by practising the command to let go you are in effect giving the muscles the opposite command of 'off'. It is in the conscious repetition of this command that you develop a strong enough connection to the musculature to relax when you have to face fear in your life.

After you have worked for a while in each of the three dimensions try searching for the centre in a circular movement pressing from left to forwards to right to back, gradually decreasing the concentric circles so as to combine the various dimensions simultaneously.

align the body

Balance is achieved only through correct body alignment. The feet, the legs, the trunk, the head are all important in creating and maintaining a balanced position. They are the vehicles of body force. Keeping the feet in proper relation to each other, as well as to the body, helps to maintain correct body alignment.   **Bruce Lee (1975)**

Postural muscles, structurally adapted to resist prolonged gravitational stress, generally resist fatigue. When overly stressed, however the same postural muscles become irritable, tight shortened.

Chaitow, Bradley et al. (2002)

We do not recognise to what extent the intellectual, the emotional and moving (body) functions are mutually dependent, although, at the same time, we can be aware of how much our moods and our emotional states depend on our movements and postures. If a man assumes a posture that corresponds, in him, to the feeling of grief or dejection, then within a short time he will actually feel grief or dejection. Fear, indifference, aversion and so on may be created by artificial changes of posture.   **Gurdjieff (1976: 156)**

The second exercise for Internal Meditation develops sensitivity to our verticality and its relationship with gravity. Our verticality is something that has evolved over a long time and is a fundamentally different situation to when our spine is in the horizontal position. You need to build awareness to your verticality so that in times of stress you can remain upright and because your verticality has a huge effect on your physical, mental and emotional wellbeing. When you awoke this morning your spine was horizontal to the ground where it had been participating in restorative, healing and rejuvenating functions. Then you hauled yourself into the upright position and your spine became vertical; from then on, you have been engaged in an act of balance. From a physiological point of view there are some profound changes that occur when your spine becomes vertical, for instance, your blood pressure changes, the breath mechanism is affected, and the movement of fluids around the body occurs in a dramatically different way. Our vertical spine has also had a profound effect on the evolution of our brain, especially the development of speech, but although this is a fascinating area of study I will not deal with it in any great depth at this point. However, it does help to have an appreciation of the differences between a horizontal and vertical spine.

For the most part our uprightness feels permanent, and we take it completely for granted. However, a closer inspection reveals that our ability to stand upright is anything but permanent – if our balance is disturbed then our spine will return to the horizontal position, in other words we will fall over. All processes of homeostasis take a continual input of energy and monitoring of balance to maintain them. Again, we wish to try to be 'open' to the physical reality of what is – in other words, how nature has built us – and not to use our imagination to construct an image; your verticality exists, you just need to build a deeper connection to it.

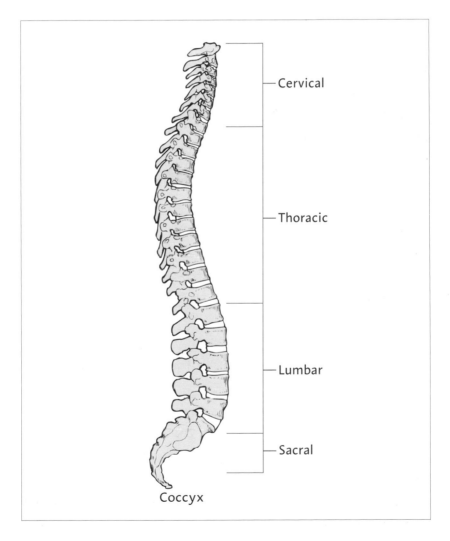

FIGURE 8

At the bottom half of our body sits a triangle. The base of the triangle is along the floor between the two feet. The two sides of the triangle are the legs, coming up at an angle to meet together at the pelvis; at exactly the point where they meet, we find the centre (Tan T'ien). On top of this triangle sits the spine, which is divided into three balanced sections: the lumbar, thoracic and cervical regions. Finally, perching on top of the spine, precisely where the primary organs of balance (the inner ear) are, is the head. These three areas: the triangular base, the spine and the head make up our basic alignment to gravity. Our arms, though important, are not essential for us to be upright. If you can build an 'inner' sensitivity to this basic shape of your alignment then your uprightness in times of stress, fear or panic will stand a much better chance of being maintained. This inner sense of alignment also plays a huge part in the overall maintenance of your health by continually monitoring and checking that the core of your body – the musculoskeletal system, which is the framework which all the other systems relate to – is as balanced as nature intended.

THE TRiANGULAR BASE

The triangular base is important because unless you are standing on one leg and hopping about, this base is always present and is what you use to move about with. Whenever you stand up the triangular base allows you to do so. The brain takes information from the left and right pressure sensitivity in the legs and maintains some form of triangle. The Basic Stance forms an equilateral triangle but generally people tend to stand with an imbalanced base, distributing their weight unequally between one leg or the other.

The feet are an incredible piece of engineering – the average footstep takes a large amount of pressure with every step – and for this reason they must be aligned in the parallel position, as in the Basic Stance, in order to function as nature intended. The vast majority of people in the Western world walk with misaligned feet; one or both of the feet are usually splayed out at uneven angles (this can be verified by looking at wear patterns on the bottom of your shoes). The foot uses a powerful system of muscles and ligaments to cope with the pressure exerted upon it; if the feet are aligned correctly then this system forms a strong arch (which is in fact another triangle between heel, arch and ball) in the foot, however, as soon as the feet start to splay this arch is weakened. If the arch begins to 'fall' your gait will be affected and this will lead to many other health problems. Every person is either right- or left-side dominant, usually corresponding to whether they are right- or left-handed – people who are right-side dominant will tend to splay the right foot out more; by meditating on the alignment of the body, we remove this fundamental imbalance.

LEFT- OR RIGHT-SIDE DOMINANT?

We take for granted the fact that everyone is either right-handed or left-handed, but how far do we see the significance of this in our life? For instance, if you are right-handed then a high percentage of every movement you make will be initiated on the right-hand side; this means that the flow of energy through the nervous system will have a propensity to move to that side more than to the left (through nerve impulses that originate in the left side of the brain). This also affects, amongst other things, our sight, hearing, breathing and coordination. In terms of musculoskeletal alignment, right-sided dominance means you are continually putting more weight down the right side of the body than the left. When our feet hit the ground as we walk, pressure waves are sent up each side of the body; when we are right-side dominant, the pressure wave will be greater on the right-hand side.

You can demonstrate this to yourself by buying a pair of foam earplugs from your local chemist, inserting them and walking around bare foot whilst listening to the sound of your feet on the ground – you will be able to hear a louder impact on the right side. Place your hand on top of your head as you walk and you should be able to feel the vibration from the foot reaching the top of your head, and next time you are with a young child place your hand lightly on top of their head when they are walking and you will feel the pressure wave going up through them. This simple exercise demonstrates the fact that a significant amount of pressure travels through the body on every step. The feet, being at the 'bottom' of the body, endure most of this pressure; if we have not been taught to walk correctly (most of us do not give a second thought to how we walk) the common tendency will be for the feet to start to splay. This is further compounded by the fact that for a large amount of time we walk on a very thin hard skin that man has deemed necessary to cover the earth with: concrete. This continual contact with a very hard substance increases the shockwaves through the body and forces the feet to splay, unfortunately slowly destroying the feet. If the feet begin to work inefficiently then the force going through the skeleton increases and, particularly as we get older, causes all sorts of musculoskeletal problems such as osteoarthritis, slipped and herniated discs in the back, neck problems, cartilage and ligament problems in the knee, and so on.

SKELETAL COMPENSATION

If the feet are not aligned correctly then the upper part of the body will compensate in some way, which will eventually create misalignment and curvature of the spine. This compensation of the body is a governing principle in osteopathy, the Alexander Technique (a now famous method of body therapy which aims to bring the body back into its natural state in accordance with nature) and pretty well every form of therapeutic bodywork. It is caused by the body trying to rebalance itself at the musculoskeletal level so, for instance, if the pelvis is tilted too far forwards then the cervical region of the spine will bend to compensate, or if the right foot is splayed out then the left hip changes its position. The original Kung Fu and T'ai Chi forms were designed to align the body equally by practising identical moves on the left and right sides of the body, bringing it back into a state of harmony (a word which in its origins actually means a 'joining or joint in proportion' and is where we get the word 'arm' from).

BIPEDAL MOTION

Returning to our triangular base, we need to discuss the fact that it uses biped motion (walking) to transport us from one place to another. On reflection one sees that when we walk, run or jump we are continually creating one triangle after another; this fact is common to all humans and is an inescapable law. Just take a moment now to recall your day up until this point and all of the places your spine has been transported to using this bipedal motion. For the most part we take this completely for granted, not even giving it a second thought, but if we injure our leg we experience just how much we depend on this triangular base to get us around and how far we take it for granted.

If the momentum of this triangle-to-triangle biped motion is interfered with, as when we trip, then we will fall. Fear or over-excitement can also destabilize the triangular base. For instance, muggers are very well-acquainted with this fact and know that when people are scared they will either freeze or try to run. Knowing that uprightness is destabilized when running, they wait for you to run and then come up from behind and push you forwards to the ground, face down and helpless, where they can come down on top of you. One other factor that contributes to this destabilization is that as one triangle moves to another triangle there is a point where gravity takes over and you literally fall towards the ground *(see The Law of Momentum, page XXX)*. If you are tripped or you slip, the momentum will continue to travel downwards taking you with it. Developing sensitivity to the moment that gravity takes over can help in keeping us upright.

The triangular base of our body brings us a sense of stability and groundedness and again, through the Principle of Resonation *(see page 26)*, will begin to create these qualities in the mind and emotions. It also allows us to transport the spine and head; that we build a connection to it is crucial for holistic self-defence.

THE ART OF WALKiNG

Walking is a form of exercise that we engage in every day, yet most of us have never given much thought, let alone practice, to the technique of walking. This is unfortunate as correct walking is a valuable and easily accessible tool to strengthen your homeostasis. Outlined below are some of the key elements to refining your walking technique.

1   Keep your feet parallel. This ensures correct alignment of the feet, which in turn aligns the knees and hips, thus strengthening the ligaments and tendons as nature intended.

2   Extend your ankle joint as you push through your stride. This helps to pump the blood back up to the heart, lessens the force being taken through the musculoskeletal system and keeps the ankle joint supple thus improving your footwork and reducing chances of ankle injuries.

3   Keep the movements of the arms balanced and relaxed. Your arms swing backwards and forwards in a counterbalancing motion to your leg movements; keeping them free and balanced allows you to walk more efficiently, using less energy, promoting correct breathing and keeping the shoulders and spine supple and relaxed.

4   Be aware of the three adjustments of the spine as outlined in the alignment section (see page 71). This ensures that the force travelling through the spine as you walk is dissipated equally over the whole skeleton.

5   Use a focus point as much as possible when walking. This helps to keep correct posture and stops the head from continually moving about, thus pulling your spine out of alignment.

ALIGNMENT OF THE SPINE

The spine, sitting on top of the triangular base, is the core of the body. We can lose a leg or arm and still survive but we cannot survive if our spine is severed. Our spine is the central framework from which the majority of our internal organs work from and if it comes out of alignment then our body is weakened at the core. From time to time we all talk about bad posture and admonish ourselves for our poor verticality because somewhere we instinctively know that the maintenance of correct posture helps our health. Nature is an extremely precise creator; your spine has been evolved to work at an exact length. The moment we lose this exactness, for instance, by slouching or craning the neck, our bodies' overall functioning is impaired. Your internal organs are designed to work at an exact distance from each other in an exact relationship to gravity; if the spine is misaligned in any way, this relationship changes. Kuchera & Kuchera (1997) beautifully described the optimum posture as follows:

> Optimal posture is the balanced configuration of the body with respect to gravity. It depends on normal arches of the feet, vertical alignment of the ankles, and horizontal orientation (in the coronal plane) of the sacral base. The presence of an optimum posture suggests that there is perfect distribution of the body mass around the centre of gravity. The compressive force on the spinal discs is balanced by ligamentous tension: there is minimal energy expenditure from postural muscles.

Notice how this definition relates posture to gravity, mentions the arches of the feet and says that in optimum posture 'there is perfect distribution of the body mass around the centre of gravity' (the Tan T'ien). Also, that the spine is held in place by ligamentous tension and not muscular power. If we deviate from this optimal posture, disease will eventually follow. When we are young, we do not notice it, but as we get older, things begin to malfunction. Nowhere is this fact more important than the relationship between the heart and the lungs (cardiorespirology). The moment we slouch, our breathing (respiratory) and heart (cardio) muscles have to work harder and over a long period of time chronic bad posture will overload the heart and/or lungs and create a host of related problems. As we go on in our Meditation, we will see that correct posture frees the breath and allows it to drop into its Natural Breath Cycle *(see page 95)*, which allows full replenishment of oxygen in the blood and release of carbon dioxide (CO_2). Both processes in turn raise our energy level *(see Harmonization of the Body, page 93)*.

To begin aligning the spine we must first of all acquaint ourselves with the three sections of the spine that have been evolved by nature and which are recognized by both Eastern and Western anatomy: the lumbar, the thoracic and the cervical sections. The alignment of the lumbar region is governed by the pelvic tilt, the alignment of the thoracic by the positioning of the shoulders and the alignment of the cervical section by the angle of the head. When we have a misalignment in one or more of these sections and a violent force enters the body, for instance, when we are pushed, pick up something heavy or make a quick reflexive action, then that force travels through the body like a wave and will cause injury at the point of misalignment. Developing a correct sense of alignment in the spine is the best insurance policy against violent back and neck injuries.

Aligning the musculoskeletal system also promotes freedom of movement in the arms and hands. I first came across this principle during my earlier career as a classical guitarist. At one summer school I attended, my teachers, who were very forward-thinking at the time, had engaged in the services of an Alexander Technique teacher. She was employed to help us fledgling guitarists to balance and align the spine so that our hands and arms could move freely from the spine, allowing us to make all the small detailed movements necessary for the art without strain. Any misalignment in the spine creates compensatory muscle tension in the torso, shoulders and arms, thus interfering with the execution of musical passages. This freedom is equally important when studying Martial Art in order to utilize the arms and the hands in the most efficient way during technique. Moreover, this study will help *anyone* who has to perform complex manipulations under pressure, for instance, nurses/doctors and performers *(see the first Chi Kung exercise, page 151)*.

Apart from allowing your hands and arms to move freely in the martial situation, skeletal alignment also plays a huge part in your ability to judge the distance of your opponent from you. If your spine is leaning forwards or back then it gives a false impression of how far away you are from your opponent. A straight balanced spine on a stable triangular base means that your head will be kept as still as possible, which makes it much easier to judge the distance to our opponent because there will only be one moving object (their body) instead of two (yours and theirs). We will deal with this in more detail in the section on Martial Science.

ALIGNMENT OF THE HEAD

The head sits on top of the spine and has to be maintained mostly in a level position. It is sometimes referred to as the second Tan T'ien as it has a centre of gravity all of its own. Any of you who have ever held someone's head in your hands will know that it is a very heavy object. The head has been evolved to balance on top of the spine and uses a complex system of muscles and ligaments to hold its poise. If it begins to lean forwards, back or to the sides it starts to pull everything else out of alignment and, due to its heaviness, requires a lot of energy in the form of muscular tension to hold it in place.

Misalignment of the head causes many problems such as impaired breathing, poor eyesight, headaches, and nerve and neck problems. The angle of the head also affects our relationship with the inner ear. It is here, where the skull hinges to the spine, that the inner ear sits making an incredible number of calculations per second just to keep us upright. If the angle of the head is chronically misaligned then it affects our ability to balance at a very deep level because the inner ear controls not only our sense of balance but also our sense of proportion, orientation to three-dimensional space and judgment of interval in sound.

The importance of the stability of the head when defending oneself against an actual physical attack cannot be emphasized enough as it is probably the single biggest factor leading to the disintegration of technique and your upright structure. If the head is not kept focused and steady then disorientation will soon occur, similar to what you feel when you get dizzy. Physiologically, the reason for this is that the fluid in the semicircular canals of the inner ear is being 'shaken' by the violent movement associated with physical confrontation. These agitated messages from the inner ear are then distorted by the rising energy in the body. One of the body's principal reactions when it perceives a threat coming towards it is a jerking back of the head and often a closing of the eyes. If you recall a time in your life where this has happened then you will remember the absolute reflexive nature of this response. The heaviness of the head means that it has a lot of momentum when it reacts in this manner; this momentum then pulls the spine out of alignment, which destroys the placement of the Tan T'ien and we lose our balance (see the first Chi Kung exercise, page 151). Similarly, the head will tend to lean forwards when applying force to something – a symptom of this is what is commonly known as 'tunnel vision' (see the second Chi Kung exercise, page 154). These two reactions – one

Yin (contracting away), one Yang (expanding towards) – are two of the most crucial factors in a conflict situation as they destroy our sense of distance and our upright structure extremely quickly. However, with correct training we can learn how to lessen their effects and to move the head out of the way or apply force without losing alignment. This is accomplished by initiating movement from the physical rather than the intellectual Tan T'ien (the head).

To return to our basic shape of triangular base, spine and head it would help also to understand the structure from the head down. Gravity enters the top back part of the head. It then travels through the head and down the spine to the Tan T'ien, and here the force of gravity is split into two and travels down each of the legs and through each foot to the ground. This may seem rather obvious but it is the *sensation* of this that is significant for us. For a long time humans thought the world was flat and we took this fact for granted; then came the revelation that the earth was in fact round and we had to rebalance our perception (homeostasis) of ourselves in relation to Mother Earth. In many ways, humans still have a tendency to think that the earth is flat and that we are actually standing on top of something. When we stand up we could be sideways or upside down, the point is that we are being held to the centre of the planet by the force of gravity. This force is channelled through our skeleton and is the same force that pulls the spine horizontal to the ground when we lose our balance. Moreover, our musculature has been evolved to work in relation to this force (remember Kuchera & Kuchera quoted on page 70) so we really need to take it into consideration whenever we move, exercise, or practice Martial Art techniques. The only way to do this is to build a sensitivity, connection and appreciation of this natural law, and then the force of gravity can act as an ally instead of something to be struggled against.

There are certain things that interfere with our ability to remain upright. Anyone who has had just a little too much alcohol to drink will have experienced this. Other significant things that impair the functioning of the inner ear are: a blocking of the sinuses, particularly the Eustachian tubes, with mucus; anything that causes a redistribution of blood to the head or the opposite, for instance, when we stand up too quickly; a decreasing input from the senses, especially the sense of sight; and most importantly for us, when we have the energy of fear in the body. Because our balance or alignment is in fact fragile we need to build sensitivity to the way our skeleton has been aligned by nature to stand upright in the face of gravity. Here is something I witnessed quite recently that seemed to express something profound about the fragility of our uprightness. I was at a children's fair and, whilst talking to one of the parents there, I looked directly down at the top of the head of their child who was about 18 months old. The child was swaying backwards, forwards, left and right, trying to stay upright, and seeing it from that perspective really illustrated the process that a young 'toddler' goes through in order to evolve a sense of balance – it was a continual movement of balance and counterbalance and the child's central core was just strong enough to measure this rebalancing. Then the child took a tentative step using the triangular base, and the balancing continued; a few more steps and you could see the phase of the balancing getting larger until the child fell back on their bottom, but then almost immediately the toddler rolled forwards and got back up again, and so it went on. It was fascinating to watch this very natural exploration into uprightness and balance, this 'conscious repetition' *(see page 149)* to develop the skill of balancing. On my way home from the fair I stopped at a supermarket to pick up some food and while standing at the checkout I noticed the person in front of me was buying a rather large amount of alcohol. When I looked at him he was searching in his wallet for money but was having difficulty because his body was swaying all over the place and his eyes were having tremendous difficulty balancing themselves in order to focus on the money in his wallet. He certainly did not need to be buying any more alcohol! These two experiences, apart from being quite amusing because of their close proximity to each other, seem to illustrate two directions: firstly the creation of a sense of alignment, and secondly the destruction of it. Incidentally, I left the man at the checkout trying very hard to open the plastic shopping bags and did not wait to see if he too ended up on his bottom – no doubt if he did he would not be as quick as the toddler to get back up again!

It would be good here to talk briefly about atmospheric pressure, which is of course created by the force of gravity. As mentioned previously, our bodies have been evolved by nature in a very exact manner, under certain laws that we cannot escape from. Our bodies have been evolved to work in this particular place on the planet and if we were to propel our bodies upwards into the atmosphere, soon the environment would become fatal for us – the temperature drops to an intolerable level, the oxygen level in the atmosphere is insufficient to sustain us, but more importantly in terms of our understanding of skeletal alignment, as the atmospheric pressure weakens, our bones begin to separate at the joints. You can verify this with any astronaut you next happen to meet, and they will tell you that if you stay in space for a prolonged period you will need to perform certain exercises to mimic the force of gravity in order to counteract this.

It may appear that I have digressed slightly from our overriding theme of self-defence. But then what happens to our skeletal alignment when we feel depressed? When we become stressed?

When we are shocked by a sudden loud sound? And what does it mean to be spineless? To have no backbone? To lose one's head? Or to not keep one's feet on the ground? Our skeletal alignment and its harmonization within the natural laws that it falls under is one of the keys to 'keeping it together' in times of stress or when we get 'upset'. There is a reason why the popular sayings 'to be spineless' and 'to stand up to somebody' are used. Again we return to a principle at the very heart of authentic Kung Fu, which is that by working through the body to harmonize and strengthen it we affect the other main energies in the body, namely the mind and the emotions. By learning how to stand up straight physically we will learn to do so emotionally as well. And learning through sensation what it means to be balanced will affect the way we think and feel. The beauty of this is that the human body is a physical tangible organism and much more accessible than our somewhat elusive thought processes and emotional response.

THE ALiGNMENT EXERCiSE

Part One

1 *Stand in the Basic Stance.*

2 *Open to the alignment of the feet. Allow the weight to come a little forwards onto the balls of the feet but do not allow the heels to come off the ground.*

3 *Sense the triangular base; try to imagine the triangle with its apex at the Tan T'ien.*

4 *Sense the angles of the ankles, knee joints and hips; try to sense the 'concertina' effect of these angles that provide you with a system of suspension.*

5 *Tuck the pelvis in and forwards but do not force it. You should feel the lower back (lumbar region) stretch.*

6 *Move your attention to the thoracic region of the spine and gently pull the shoulders back until you feel gravity pulling down on the arms. If you have difficulty with this then try doing the 'tiger claw' exercise (see page 158).*

7 *Without losing sensation from the lower body bring your attention to the head and neck area and adjust the angle of the head by pushing the head up from the top back part of the head. To help you represent this imagine being pulled up by a thread from this area.*

8 *Direct the attention through the whole alignment process from the feet up through the legs and spine to the top of the head. Whilst sensing the aligned structure, gradually allow your head to tilt forwards, feeling it affect your uprightness (it pulls the whole body forwards). Then allow it to tilt backwards; again sense its effects (you can also do this moving the head sideways, when you should feel the pressure increasing down the side of the body you moved the head to).*

9 *Try to see in the mind's eye the upright structure, the triangular base, the spine and the head but do not include the arms.*

Part Two

1   *Sense gravity entering in through the top back part of the head.*
2   *From there, follow it down the spine paying attention again to our three sections and corresponding adjustments.*
3   *Feel the weight splitting at the Tan T'ien.*
4   *Follow the energy down the legs and out of the feet to the ground.*
5   *Do parts one and two one after the other, moving up and then down the body.*
6   *Try to feel parts one and two simultaneously.*

It is important in this exercise to sense your alignment from the ground upwards (Yang) and then from the head down to the ground (Yin). The Chinese taught that there is one force holding us to the ground (gravity) and one that is pushing us away (due to the Earth's rotation). This connection to your alignment can also be found in your normal standing position and not just in the Basic Stance. It is also helpful to try to find alignment when you are in the sitting position, utilizing the pelvis as your base.

Aligning the body allows the Intelligent Warrior to stand upright in front of physical, mental and emotional pain and fear, thus enabling you to gain a clear, accurate impression of the perceived threat.

the definition of the body

The transition from totally uncoordinated
muscular effort to skill of the highest perfection is
a process of developing the connections in the
nervous system.   Lee (1975)

In the introduction to Meditation we started to discuss the idea that
we in fact have two bodies – the physical body and the body of
attention – an idea that has been expressed in many different
teachings throughout the ages. The physical body is rooted in the
present moment and it cannot bend the laws of time and space, whilst
our body of attention can enter into the present moment but also has
the ability to project into the future and the past, in other words it can
daydream about past or future experiences. An example of the body of
attention and the physical body coming apart is when you have seen
somebody or felt yourself 'staring off into space', eyes glazed over,
looking at something in the 'mind's eye', not hearing when your name
is called, and so on. The practice of defining the body aims to bring the
body of attention into the same shape as that of the physical body,
melding them together into a balanced whole. For this to happen we
must bring the body of attention into the present moment and to do

this we must understand the mechanics of attention.

As you sit here reading your attention is being used for the task – a certain amount of bioelectricity is being used to make the necessary connections for the writing on the page to be received by the senses and translated into thought. This process of reading was developed at an early age and is now so well 'embodied' that you do not have to think about it, all you need to do is to direct your attention towards the page. You then have to continue to 'pay' attention to the page in order to comprehend the words, sentences, paragraphs and chapters smoothly (remember the example given in the introduction to Meditation of reading without attention). So first there is an intention to do something and then a maintaining of attention in order to stay the distance and complete the task. This presupposes the fact that we have a degree of control over what we call our attention and it is here that things become extremely relevant for the Intelligent Warrior for the body of attention is the single most important factor in developing awareness and presence. In order to illustrate this further try this simple exercise:

1   Gain a sense of how you are now, whatever that means to you.
2   Direct your attention to your left foot.
3   Without losing the awareness of your left foot, sense the right foot.
4   Next, become aware of your tongue.
5   Return to your original sense of yourself but include the deeper impressions of the two feet and the tongue.

From this simple exercise we can see something that is actually quite profound. By directing our attention towards a certain part of our body we can then receive a more detailed impression of that area – there is a *connection* via our *attention* originating from an *intention* from the mind. In other words, you read my instructions and hopefully followed them by directing your attention to where I asked. In return, you received a more detailed impression of your body as it was in that moment. The body of attention at that moment was slightly closer to the shape of your physical body, they were slightly more 'together' and perhaps you had at that moment a stronger individuality or 'indivisible-duality'. As a further experiment try to hold this connection with your feet and tongue as you read the rest of this section.

From a physiological point of view, the system that we will be developing in this section is the nervous system. This extraordinary controlling system allows the free flow of communication through the body by using a form of bioelectricity that travels at approximately 400 metres per second and can work on a purely unconscious level using the autonomic nervous system or on a conscious level engaging the somatic nervous system. Briefly, the autonomic nervous system is mainly concerned with maintaining the automatic functions (without deliberate mental or other effort on our part) of organs such as the heart, lungs, stomach, intestine, bladder, sex organs and blood vessels. It consists entirely of motor nerves arranged in relays from the spinal cord to the various muscles. It is divided into two parts – the sympathetic and the parasympathetic – that work in balance to turn various processes on and off (Yin and Yang). An area of the brain called the hypothalamus controls the autonomic nervous system. This receives information about any variations in, for instance, the body's chemical make up and adjusts the autonomic system to bring the body back into the right balance (homeostasis). The somatic system has a dual role. First, it collects information about the outside world from sensory organs such as the eyes, which is then communicated to the appropriate part of the brain. Second, it transmits signals through motor fibres from the central nervous system to the skeletal muscles, thus initiating movement. It is not within the scope of this book to delve deeply into the physiological explanations of how these systems work but I would urge anyone who is not familiar with them to take the time to study their basic workings.

The autonomic and somatic nervous systems, although separate, work together and are continually affecting each other. This is of tremendous significance for our study of holistic self-defence. If by our practice of Meditation we can use the conscious direction of energy (the attention) via the somatic nervous system to communicate to the hypothalamus (autonomic) that the body is not under threat, then we can counteract the chemical reactions of fear in the body (this process is sometimes known as biofeedback). The fight-or-flight response brings us a major boost of energy and natural drugs to help us in a conflict situation. For that reason, we do not want to actually inhibit it when faced with a challenging situation, but if we have not built an awareness to fear then as this energy rushes into the body it will severely disrupt the workings of our somatic nervous system, in other words our conscious direction of attention (this of course will destroy any technique you try to employ), and also some of the finer functions from the autonomic system such as our ability to balance and breathe. Incidentally, are you still connected to your feet and your tongue? If you are, well done, retain that connection. If you are not, at what point did you lose the connection? Also, when I reminded you about it, what happened? Did that detailed impression reappear?

The process of defining the body involves (with our intention) directing the attention to various parts of the body and then holding or maintaining it there in order to strengthen the neural connections between our mind (the source of our intention) and our bodies (the target of our intention). You have already started to use this process in this manner when you centred and aligned the body, however, in the definition of the body you are working more closely with the direct sensation of certain parts of your body via its controlling and sensing systems. The somatic system is an excellent example of Yin and Yang: with our intention we send our attention to a specific part of the body (Yang) where we receive the impression of that part of the body which flows back to the mind (Yin). In esoteric Kung Fu this was termed as an 'orbit'. An orbit may be seen in modern-day terms as a biofeedback loop, in that we are trying to maintain a continual connection to a certain area of our body in order to gain a degree of control over it. The strength of the connection will determine the amount of control and most importantly our ability to access that control in times of stress. Let us now look at some of the areas that it would be beneficial to build a connection to.

THE FIVE POINTS OF COORDINATION

The five points of coordination are the physical points that our body uses to map and control our overall movements: the two feet, two hands and the head. They are also the physical extremities from the Tan T'ien (the reason why frostbite first occurs in the feet, hands, nose and ears). The cerebellum (a small part of the brain that hangs off the back of the cerebrum and controls the coordination and smooth execution of movements whose neural connections are approximately 20 times as dense as that of the cerebrum) uses the five points and their relation to the Tan T'ien to coordinate movement. It has the ability to store and recall movements 'holisticly', that is to say of all five points simultaneously.

This is very different to the control that the cerebrum or intellectual centre exerts, for the cerebrum tends to be only able to track one of the points at any time. The understanding of this led Bruce Lee to write:

> The consciousness of self is the greatest hindrance to the proper execution of all physical action. **Lee (1975: 7)**

By this Lee meant that the moment we think about a technique it interferes with the functioning of the cerebellum. In its use of the five points, the cerebellum employs a balanced relationship between manifestation (Yang) and transition (Yin).

Manifestation is the actual technique at the moment of application, for instance, the moment a Front Kick *(see page 192)* impacts upon the target and actually becomes a Front Kick. Transition, on the other hand, is the pathway the body has travelled to reach the technique so the move from, say, a punch to a kick. To reach a technique the body has to change its shape but at some point it stops changing shape and actually becomes a recognizable technique. This could be applied to any movement we make. For instance, you are reading this book (with of course awareness of your two feet and your tongue!) and your body suggests that it might be a good time for a cup of tea, so you dissolve the technique of reading and begin to walk towards the kettle (transition). The moment that you touch the kettle, you 'manifest' the technique of making a cup of tea. It is important to understand the relationship between manifestation and transition because we need to keep a connection with the five points of coordination through both. There is a tendency in humans, especially in Western society (being somewhat materially based), to focus on the manifestation or 'thing' rather than the transition or the 'no-thing'. A symptom of this is the increasing emphasis put on flashy or 'secret' techniques that are advertised in the Martial Art press and by various schools to attract more fee-paying students (you could of course apply this to the advertising of any product). The essence of Martial Art lies, as always, in the balance between actual technique (manifestation) and one's ability to find the correct technique in movement (transition) to adapt to the situation. Next time you watch your favourite sport try to see the principle of transition and manifestation – the tennis player returning to the centre of the court between each stroke or the golfer preparing, stepping up to the ball and then 'executing' the stroke; slow motion on television is excellent for this.

In the Defining the Body exercise *(see page 81)* we will open and build a connection (intention) to the five points of coordination in order to evolve a deeper more permanent connection to them (target). Using your intention, you will connect to them and then receive the impression back, allowing it to flow up into the cerebellum. If you apply the concept of conscious repetition *(see page 149)* to this process your connection will become increasingly robust so that in times of extreme conflict, such as a physical attack or having to apply first aid at a crash scene, your connection with manifestation and transition will remain intact. It is the continual flow of information that allows the cerebellum to calculate and coordinate our movements. We are, if you like, strengthening the internal 'wiring' structure that leads directly to the cerebellum, bypassing the analysis processes of the cerebrum or intellectual functions. Without a stable centre it is very difficult for the cerebellum to understand the relationship between these five points. If, however, our centre is strong then, like planets orbiting the sun, our hands, feet and head will have an exact relationship

The Intelligent Warrior

with the centre and our movements will become smooth and coordinated. On a lighter note, imagine what this kind of practice would do for your golf handicap or tennis game, especially in times of stress such as during a competition!

To recap, the cerebellum likes to remember movement in a holistic manner. It holds the memory of the movement as a whole so that the movement can be triggered as one unit and not as singular instructions *(see The Process of Embodiment, page 145)*. It likes to send the instruction to the various parts of your body simultaneously so that when you move from one technique to another the move is done smoothly and follows into the second seamlessly.

When your body perceives an imminent attack, be it physical, mental or emotional, it instantaneously initiates the fight-or-flight response. One of the first things to suffer when this happens is the connection to your five points. The symptoms of this tend to be one of two things: either the body will freeze (or in less intense situations movements will become stiff) so that even though the brain might tell the feet to run, the feet will not obey; or a person will overreact, wildly throwing their arms and legs about without much control. The overriding sensation of the fight-or-flight response is that the energy released in the body travels upwards. This 'logjams' the information flowing up into and out of the brain, severely disrupting communication and subsequently destroying coordination. The feet being furthest away are one of the first things to lose connection, along with your manual dexterity. This is beautifully illustrated by one of the first reactions of a young baby when it becomes startled by, for instance, a loud sound. When this occurs the baby will immediately fling its arms and legs outwards away from the centre. This most instinctual of reactions is hard-wired into us by nature and still plays a regular part in our daily lives.

Once we lose control of the five points, our ability to balance and stay upright, let alone apply a technique, becomes virtually nonexistent. The power of this reaction is illustrated well by an experience I had during the time I was a bouncer in London. During one of my shifts a group of rowdy, young football supporters were celebrating with great enthusiasm at a corner table in the bar I was working at. As time (marked by the flow of beer) went on they became an increasing nuisance to staff and customers alike so I went and stood by the bar pretending to read a newspaper whilst actually observing them using peripheral vision. The use of peripheral vision in these cases is invaluable for gathering information before engaging directly with an opponent. It did not take long for them to notice me and it was plain that they were hatching a plot to have some fun. Soon one of them broke away from the pack and started to approach me from behind in order, I found out later, to try and scare me from behind, no doubt by grabbing me and yelling 'boo'. Unfortunately for my would-be assailant, he was still at the edge of my peripheral awareness and just as he was about to pounce, I turned, raised my hands, grimaced and let out a roar of comical proportions. The shock of this surreal image entering his body made him snap his head back, lose balance, stumble and finally land on a somewhat large part of his anatomy, without me ever touching him. His friends fell about with laughter and the embarrassment was too much for this 'barroom ninja' and he retired red-faced to console himself with his beer. After I had enquired as to the purpose of his actions, we all became quite good friends. On reflection, I remember being quite 'struck' by the incident, that just an impression could knock a man (and a large one at that) off his feet.

A characteristic of the instinctual fight-or-flight reaction is that it takes over control of the body, mind and emotions instantaneously. This was illustrated to me very clearly in the following incident.

A customer in the bar had been getting increasingly lewd with the waitresses, so the management asked me to remove him. He was a very large man and so the proposition of getting him out of the crowded bar was a tricky one. He was seated in a large, comfy chair and was trying to lift the waitresses' skirts up with his foot as they came by. I approached him, explained the situation and was rewarded with a foulmouthed response and an assurance that he was not going to be moved from his chair. With this he seemed to sink lower into his chair and settle himself in. To try to drag this ugly bulk of a man up out of his chair seemed a rather unsavoury task, so leaning over I slapped him playfully around both cheeks and told him he was a 'very naughty boy'. Immediately the blood rushed up into his face, his body tensed and venom shot from his eyes. Once again I slapped him, but this time with slightly more force. The addition of pain into his already humiliated state was too much for him and, much to my satisfaction, he hauled his bulk out of the chair. Once upright, he proceeded to throw a lumbering right hook, which I answered with a Twist Punch *(see page 196)* and another slap, simultaneously telling him that he was now a 'very, very naughty boy'. By this time, several of the customers who had witnessed this somewhat amusing 'bull-baiting' were beginning to giggle in the background, which further enraged him. Once again he came at me with an identical right punch; my answer was the same but harder and he stumbled backwards. I could see by the look in his eyes that he was beginning to 'crumble inwardly'; he nervously looked at some of the amused spectators, realizing that he looked a bit of 'turkey'. So, what does he do now? Rather astonishingly, he sits down on the ground, crosses his arms stares, straight ahead and refuses to reply to any of my requests for him to leave. Indicating to the barman that I was in need of his assistance, we both took hold of one of his arms and picked him up off the ground. Unbelievably, he tried to keep his legs in the sitting position; he did not struggle but stayed as best he could in his frozen posture whilst we carried him outside and put him politely on the pavement. He immediately got up and tried to hit me again with exactly the same right hook. My response? The same slap to his face, but this time with some anger in it because I was getting a bit annoyed. He reeled back then started to come in once again. However, as I made just the slightest gesture to slap him he realized, before throwing his punch, that the same conclusion was inevitable. Turning on his heels he stalked off and muttered something about calling the police. But that, I am very glad to say, was the last I ever saw of him. This story illustrates very well the power of reaction in the body; one second my friend was adamant that he would not be moving and the next, after the slap and emotional taunt caused the energy to rise in his body, he was standing on his feet. It is also interesting to note that he threw the same attack four times, which is very common when the body is in shock; oddly enough, so is the freezing of posture seen when he tried to remain in a sitting position whilst we carried him out.

The skill developed in defining the body counterbalances rising energy, but it does not suppress it as we need the energy that the fight-or-flight response gives us. However, what we are aiming to do is to channel this energy through the body so that it becomes a powerful ally. A good example of this can be found in performance. For instance, an experienced musician will channel the nervous energy they feel before a performance so that it actually makes them perform better, whereas an inexperienced musician will be debilitated by the nervous reaction in the body. The key to channelling this instinctive reaction is to create a strong enough body of attention that can consciously relax the physical body and direct the attention to the five points. Relaxing or 'letting go' is the principal communication from our minds to our bodies, and the movement of relaxation allows the free flow of energy, whether

          The Intelligent Warrior

that is the blood supply, hormones or neural instructions. So, when we talk about the mechanics of attention, relaxation is the fundamental skill behind it. For instance, the sensation of your feet is here now, you do not have to invent it, all you have to do is intend your attention towards the area and open (the movement of relaxation) to the sensation coming back up again. The moment we tense it becomes more difficult for the body to communicate with itself; it is quite easy to understand that in relation to the flow of blood, but it is also the same for neural commands.

Defining the body allows the Intelligent Warrior to channel the bioelectrical impulses elicited by shock away from your brain, ensuring a continual flow of coordinated movement and keeping your head clear to make informed decisions.

THE EXERCISE OF DEFINING THE BODY

1 *In the Basic Stance, with the eyes closed gently, direct your attention towards your feet. Receive the impression and sense that you are both intending and receiving.*

2 *Try to sense each connection as an orbit – a continuous loop of intention towards each foot and receiving the impression back up again.*

3 *Without losing connection with the feet, try the same process with the hands. Using relaxation, Intend your attention towards the hands and receive the impression, then try to sense the orbits again.*

4 *Balance your attention between the feet and hands and try to feel all four points as equal.*

5 *Open to the sensation of your face, relaxing any tensions you might find there, especially around the forehead and the eyes.*

6   Hold all five points with your attention; try simultaneously to become aware of the Tan T'ien.
7   Try to see in your 'mind's eye' the five points placed around your centre, but do not allow this to become more powerful than your physical sensation.

The key to this exercise is relaxation. Remember that the sensation of the target of your intention, such as your foot, is always there. You do not have to invent it, just gently open the neural pathways and allow the sensation to flow into your mind. Spend a little bit of time with each target before moving on to the next. Be very attentive to the interference from internal conversation for it will pull the energy into your head and break the connection with your body. Move on to the Advanced Meditation section only after you have become adept at this exercise. It may appear very simple 'to do' this exercise at first, but it is actually the depth of connection rather than the complexity of the exercise that counts.

the harmonization
of the body

The basic principle of the training, that inside and outside join, enables people to gradually attain intercourse and merging of the totality of body and mind. The special training of consciousness and the respiratory system, gradually advancing, effectively regulates every system of the mechanical body as well as the technical capacities of the whole being; it regulates the entire nervous system and endocrine system and at the same time gradually leads to a higher level of harmony and integration of the self with the external world (including both nature and society).
Shi Ming (1994: xix)

Precise regulation of respiration is crucial to health, but many things can go wrong. Breathing is subject to major interference and disruption, in large part because of thinking, feeling, and experience, and also as a result of biomechanical and biochemical factors. **Chaitow (2002: 9)**

The human body (our 'instrument') is an extremely complex, miraculous piece of biotechnology; its systems work together to ensure the maintenance of homeostasis. In this chapter we will look at the process that allows the synchronization between the bodily systems to take place: breathing. As you are reading this now, gently become aware of your breath, reflect upon the fact that the average human breathes between 14,000 and 22,000 times in a 24-hour cycle and that you have been breathing since the day you were born and will continue until you die. How many of these countless breaths have you been aware of? How much do you know about, let alone practice, the correct, natural breathing technique? In every Meditation system I have ever studied (systems originating from all over the planet and at different times in man's history), the awareness of the breath and consequent refinement of the breathing technique plays a pivotal role. Good breathing habits are fundamental to the maintenance of health in the body and allow an exchange of gases involving the acquisition of oxygen (O_2) and the elimination of carbon dioxide (CO_2). The efficient exchange of these gases enhances cellular function and so facilitates normal performance of the brain, organs and body tissues. The breath synchronizes our bodily systems via a complex set of reflexes – it assists in fluid movement (lymph, blood) and helps maintain spinal mobility through regular, mobilizing, thoracic cage movement. It enhances digestive function via rhythmic positive and negative pressure fluctuations. Of course, bad breathing habits will adversely affect all of the above.

Breathing plays a vital role in maintaining the homeostasis between the physical, intellectual and emotional energies in the body and has a profound effect on how we express ourselves. For instance, musical phrases all have their origins in breathing, and you speak on the 'out' breath and replenish on the 'in' breath, the process of which has played a fundamental part in forming our thought processes. Even popular advice, such as 'take a few deep breaths' which is given before entering into a stressful situation, points to an understanding of the role that breath plays in harmonizing and keeping us balanced. In a self-defence situation against actual physical attack, control of breath brings increased power, stamina, freedom of movement and the ability to control the debilitating effects of fear.

THE NATURAL BREATH CYCLE

In the previous sections on Meditation we strove to understand our bodies in terms of how nature has evolved us. Through the process of relaxation we have found the natural centre of gravity and the natural alignment of the skeletal frame, and have built a connection through the nervous system to our body. Now, through the same process, we allow the breath cycle to find its natural rhythm. There are many teachings that expound different techniques of breathing. However, to change your breath cycle is to radically interfere with the timing of your body. As your breath goes round its cycle it fires various reflexes that tell the other systems where they are, and this allows the brain stem to monitor and adjust our homeostasis. Even if your breathing might be out of balance normally, it is still what your body knows as balance so be very careful about bringing artificial breath techniques to your 'normal' breath cycle. If you have ever listened to someone (especially a child) fall asleep at night, then you will have heard the Natural Breath Cycle, and if you have ever felt your breathing relax upon getting into a hot shower then you will have experienced the movement towards the Natural Breath Cycle. Sometimes, when we witness a beautiful work of art or sunset, our breath is 'taken away'. This is followed by a reharmonization into the Natural Breath Cycle, which in turn engenders a profound sense of connection with ourselves, the world around us, and ultimately the universe and our place in it. When we relax, the breathing naturally drops down significantly towards the Tan T'ien, which immediately stimulates the diaphragm and core abdominal muscles to start powering the breath. And if we then replace breathing through the mouth with breathing through the nose we have the basis for breathing as nature intended.

The primary physiological function of breathing is its role in allowing the body and atmosphere to exchange gases, involving the acquisition of oxygen and the elimination of carbon dioxide; the efficient exchange of these gases enhances cellular function. Briefly, oxygen absorbed from the air via the lungs into the bloodstream is carried around the body nourishing and energizing the cells. It then picks up waste products from the cells and carries them back (in the form of carbon dioxide) to the lung for expellation. If we do not breathe correctly then the cells do not get the necessary food and many harmful toxins remain in the bloodstream. Oxygen is the one substance more than any other that the body needs for the maintenance of health – many of the common diseases we see rising in society now are due to oxygen depletion. However, it is very easy with our Western mindset of good and bad to see oxygen as 'good' and carbon dioxide as 'bad' when the body actually needs a *balance* between the two gases – a deficiency of carbon dioxide can cause fainting, seizures or even death.

Traditionally both Western and Eastern medicine recognize that there are two kinds of breathing: diaphragmatic and intercostal. The Natural Breath Cycle is based on diaphragmatic breathing; intercostal breathing is largely a symptom of stress and involves breathing through the mouth and with the upper part of the lung.

The Intelligent Warrior

Unfortunately, intercostal breathing is the most common among humans. Intercostal breathing is also related to the most common form of breathing problem in times of stress: hyperventilation. As discussed earlier, when the fight-or-flight reaction occurs, energy travels upwards causing intercostal breathing, which tends to trigger hyperventilation.

HYPERVENTiLATiON

Hyperventilation is by far the most common breathing disorder yet it is difficult to 'pin down' because it can be present in varying degrees of acuteness. It is characterized by an increased frequency of breath through the mouth, intercostal breathing and a disintegration of focus. Some of you may have experienced the effects of hyperventilation, while others will have a milder form and not know that it operates in their lives. Hyperventilation tends to occur when we lose a mental grasp on a situation (in colloquial terms when we 'lose it'). It is very closely related to phobias such as the fear of heights and the fear of flying.

Interestingly, the first description of hyperventilation in Western medical literature was recorded in times of conflict. It dates back to the USA during the civil war when a surgeon studied 300 soldiers who were suffering from breathlessness, dizziness, palpitations and chest pain; the symptoms improved when the soldiers were removed from the front line of battle. Subsequent research has shown that hyperventilation disrupts almost all of the body systems; some of the effects relevant to self-defence are numbness and tingling in the extremities, dizziness, tremors, blurred and tunnel vision, anxiety, palpitations, limb weakness and nausea. Hyperventilation causes a fundamental imbalance in the body, and is much like playing a musical instrument that is severely out of tune or driving a car that has not been serviced. We are most susceptible to hyperventilation when we are under attack or when we *perceive* something as a threat, perhaps because of a phobia. A student of mine once found out he was claustrophobic when locked into a pod with his family at the top of the London Eye (a popular London tourist attraction resembling an extremely tall Ferris wheel, where groups of people travel round slowly in enclosed pods). His breathing became fast and shallow, his heart was palpitating and he broke out into a cold sweat. His two young children, through the Principle of Resonation *(see page 26)*, began to panic upon sensing his agitation. Luckily, his *awareness* alerted him to what was happening and he was able to regain some *presence* by shutting his eyes and encouraging the return of his Natural Breath Cycle. This did not stop the claustrophobia completely but it did allow him to control the fear's energy enough to finish the ride (which took about 15 minutes) with his eyes closed and to calm his family with a controlled voice. The poor man then took the underground home and started to have another attack on the train!

THE CHiNESE PERSPECTiVE

Eastern medicine's overriding perspective is that the breath acts as a timing mechanism. Making a physiological connection between the head (the intellectual centre) and the Tan T'ien (the physical centre), it forms the 'primary orbit'. In between the head and the Tan T'ien lies the third centre – the emotional centre – which has its physical home in the solar plexus. As the breath is drawn from the atmosphere through the nose, it travels down past the solar plexus to the Tan T'ien, then travels back up again and is returned, transformed, to the atmosphere. As the breath moves round its cycle, it triggers the spine to fire a wave of reflexes. In Chinese medicine the concept of breathing encompasses much more than our narrow Western viewpoint, and this is reflected in the different definitions of 'lung' in both traditions:

> The Chinese lung and the Western lung share some similarity. They both relate to the intake of air and include some of the same physical structures. But the Chinese concept takes the physical organs as only one component of a larger functional group, which includes the process of extracting Chi from the environment in the form of air, circulating Chi along with fluids, and (offering) overall body protection. The lung, then, is involved with fluid metabolism and transportation in the Chinese concept. It moves fluids down to the kidney and around the body especially the skin and pores. The relationship to the skin includes the body hair and sweat glands, and the secretion of sweat. Finally the lung is related to protection from 'external invasion' seen in traditional Chinese medicine to include both infection and climatic influences
>
> Ryan & Shattuck (1994)

BODY, MIND AND SPIRIT HARMONIZATION

The exercise of connecting to the breath strengthens our ability to harmonize the body, mind and spirit in times of conflict or stress. The common advice given to somebody who is becoming angry or is about to enter a stressful situation is usually to 'take a few deep breaths'. This points to a common understanding, which is not unfounded, that the breath can help you to calm emotional agitation. Bringing your attention to your breathing and encouraging it to deepen will begin to bring about the harmonization of the somatic and autonomic nervous systems.

The breath is one of the body's few autonomic functions that can be overridden by the somatic nervous system. For example, you can hold your breath or speed it up but you cannot tell your liver or kidneys to stop working. This fact opens up a direct communication to the instinctual side of ourselves and allows us to build a working relationship, via the breath, with the fight-or-flight response.

When the body perceives a threat, the hypothalamus initiates the fight-or-flight response, and it does this with an instinctual sensitivity to the degree of danger it perceives. For example, a large unexpected bill can trigger fear in your body, but not to the same degree as an assailant that is approaching you can. In the case of the unexpected bill, the anxiety could be almost imperceptible to your conscious mind yet have a significant impact on your homeostasis by, for example, triggering mild hyperventilation. The study of Meditation trains your *awareness* to alert you to fear in your body. Therefore, if you have practised a connection to your breath then you will be able to instruct it, via the somatic nervous system, to release and drop into your Natural Breath Cycle. This will communicate to the brain stem and hypothalamus that there is no threat and your autonomic nervous system will begin to shut down the instinctual fight-or-flight response. If you maintain the connection, your physical body will begin to relax and your mind will begin to regain focus. This refocusing of the mind is significant because if you allow the mind to daydream and revert to negative images then the fight-or-flight response will begin again.

The danger to your health brought about by prolonged exposure to stress and anxiety is significant. The instinct of the fight-or-flight response is designed to protect you from life-threatening situations and not the many imagined threats that we have the luxury to indulge in in Western society. Prolonged exposure to stress and anxiety can pose a serious threat to your physiological homeostasis. Leon Chaitow writes:

> Anxiety is not merely a mental phenomenon. Perception of threat is supported by bodily changes designed to enhance readiness for action. Increased breathing is often one of those changes; it is reasonable in the short term because it creates a mild state of alkalosis. This would help offset a possible surge of acid in the blood ... But if action does not occur within a minute or two, homeostasis is disrupted. No action means no surge in CO_2 production, even though the breathing is expecting it if the perception of threat continues, the physiological alarm condition continues also, often boosted more by perception of the bodily changes, which are the shadow of the anxious thinking. The chemical cascade (and eventual imbalance) then becomes an additional disturbance to the person seeking safety by worrying and hypervigilance — the human body is not really equipped to deal with chronic anxiety.   Chaitow (2002: 68)

In the case of being physically attacked, the threats perceived by the body are much greater and the reaction in your body will increase correspondingly. Connecting to your breath in a situation such as this uses the same cooperation between the somatic and autonomic systems but will not tend to stop the reaction unless you have trained to a very high level. However, it is not necessary to stop it; indeed, the extra energy released into your body via the fight-or-flight response is useful to us, but only if you learn how to channel it for your own purposes. The first step towards this is to bring the attention onto the breath so that you can keep focused in order to prepare for the initiation of explosive movement.

Breathing and Physical Self-defence

Chi Kung deals with harmonizing the breath and movement to prepare to apply self-defence techniques (Martial Science) in conflict situations (Martial Art). A strong connection to the breathing is indispensable for keeping your focus when awaiting attack and then harmonizing the 'in' and 'out' breath to the corresponding Yin/Yang phases inherent in all correct technique. This brings a degree of integration that is not possible if the physicality of the technique is studied in isolation to the breath; a good Martial Art instructor should be able to tell you, at any second, where your breath is and where it should be located in any technique. Finding the Natural Breath Cycle and then strengthening it via the process of Chi Kung increases your chances of maintaining your Chi levels in moments of intense activity. If you do not balance the 'out' breath (which is most commonly found in actions of striking) with a correspondingly powerful 'in' breath, then soon no self-defence at all will be possible.

HARMONiZiNG THE BODY EXERCiSE

In this exercise we will follow a similar process to the centring, aligning and defining areas of Meditation. In other words, you will build a connection between your intention (mind) and the target, in this case your breath. The connection and subsequent maintenance of a connection is made via the energy of your attention.

1   *Stand in the Basic Stance, keeping a connection to the five points of coordination.*
2   *Keep your mouth closed and place your tongue gently on the hard palate just behind your front teeth.*
3   *Sense the air moving in and out through the nose.*
4   *Utilize the third dimension from the Centring the Body exercise to relax and sink your weight down towards the Tan T'ien.*
5   *Allow your abdomen to move out as you breathe in and in as you breathe out. Connect this to the sensation of the air moving in and out through the nose.*
6   *Sense your spinal alignment and try to feel the breath moving up and down the spine.*
7   *Stay in this position following the breath in and out; be especially aware of the point where the 'in' breath (Yin) turns into the 'out' breath (Yang), and vice versa.*
8   *Be mindful of any internal conversation and do not let it distract you from staying connected to the complete breath cycle.*

Always try to find the Natural Breath Cycle through relaxation and awareness of the diaphragm. If you practice finding it on a regular basis, you should be able to feel the harmonizing effects of the breath fairly immediately. If you have never done any deep-breathing exercises before, then it may take some patience and perseverance to find the Natural Breath Cycle.

The process of Inner Meditation allows the Intelligent Warrior to develop direct lines of communication with their own bodies; by so doing they gain valuable insight into the relationship between their body, mind and spirit. This insight allows the Intelligent Warrior to subtly affect the action/reaction cycle.

outer meditation

Outer Meditation involves building a connection to our vibration-sensing devices, which we know as the sense organs and which the Taoists referred to as the pathways. By building a connection to them in the same way that we build a connection to the areas of Inner Meditation, we can heighten their sensitivity or 'sense activity'.

PERiPHERAL AWARENESS

Peripheral awareness is a great potential awaiting development in human beings. It is the evolution of a more holistic perception by the senses, characterized by the ability to process both specific and nonspecific impressions simultaneously. In terms of self-defence, it is an indispensable skill that can save your life. In terms of your life, it can have profound repercussions by evolving the way you apply your senses to the reception of impressions. Peripheral awareness can be developed in any of the senses, but for our purposes we will concentrate on the following three.

The Hearing

> From the first hour, I took full responsibility for
> enrolling new members. Each new applicant was
> introduced to me, and to me alone. I talked with
> him for a long time; I directed at him that special
> look which blindness had taught me. It was much
> easier for me than for anyone else to strip him of
> all pretences. His voice expressed his inner being,
> and sometimes betrayed him.   **Lusseyran (1999: 33)**

Blinded at an early age but later to become one of the key members
of the French Resistance during World War II, Jacques Lusseyran
writes with great insight, referring to the interviews he conducted
for potential members of the French Resistance during World War II.
What he refers to as 'that special look' is the same as the seamless
web of awareness *(see page 43)* developed by the correct practice of
Meditation.

The hearing is an incredible tool for self-defence. It can search a
360-degree radius around you, making it a valuable early-warning
system. We can see it at work in a good guard dog; in the voice of
a potential assailant it can perceive subtle clues as to their
intentions; and it can help to orientate and stabilize you in the
three-dimensional space. Because of our dependency on the sense
of sight we very often ignore the 'insight' that listening can bring;
we must, like a blind person or a good musician, learn how to trust
our hearing.

Musicians know that if the laws of music are studied in a practical
way then their sense of pitch, rhythm and form will improve. They
learn how to bring their energy or attention to the ears in order to

listen with greater sensitivity. Being able to do this affects many things in the body, some of which are significant for self-defence. The inner ear helps you to orientate yourself in three-dimensional space: much like a bat sends an ultrasonic signal to discern its surroundings, human beings continually process information about the three-dimensional space by the sounds that reverberate off walls and objects. For instance, concrete walls have a very different sound to wooden ones, a room with high ceilings sounds very different to one with low ceilings, a good sound engineer will tell you that the amount of people in a room changes its acoustics, and so on. This is significant for holistic self-defence because one of the main effects of shock is disorientation, so, conversely, it stands to reason that you will be less prone to the debilitating effects of shock if you are more thoroughly orientated in your environment, via your hearing.

Developing peripheral awareness in the hearing allows you to focus on one sound while still listening to all the sounds available to you. It helps to keep hearing centred whilst reaching out to perceive, in closer detail, one particular sound. Good jazz musicians develop this talent so that they can hear the whole band, yet at the same time focus on the subtle changes in a soloist's playing. In self-defence terms, this skill allows you to keep open to your three-dimensional surroundings whilst pinpointing, for example, somebody's footsteps behind you. Utilizing the hearing can tell you how many people are following you, how heavy and tall they are, how fast they are approaching, whether they are wearing hard or soft shoes, and the direction of their step.

Becoming sensitive to your hearing plays a large part in the process of 'grounding' energy. The action/reaction cycle described earlier is very sensitive to the information received by the hearing. For instance, when you hear a particularly violent sound or exceptionally good or bad news, the reaction that follows instantaneously sends the energy upwards. When you meditate, learn to listen while staying connected to the body. The two most important connections during the process of grounding are to the feet and to the breathing. If you listen while sensing the feet and the breath then the reaction that occurs, for example, when someone screams or is verbally abusive, will be greatly diminished. Although the brain will interpret this impression as an act of aggression and trigger the fight-or-flight response, causing energy to rise in the body, if you have practised a connection with the feet then you will be able to redirect the energy downwards, which will enable you to practice nonattachment to the reaction. This is a skill that you can develop and introduce into your life – for example, if you are standing in range of a loud noise such as a bus or jackhammer try to connect with your feet and use the connection to the breath to help you relax in front of the sound.

Learning to work with your hearing also allows you to carefully listen to someone who has confronted you, so you can read the clues that their voice has to offer about their intentions. Such things as nervousness, agitation, slurring of speech and rhythmic variance can tell you whether someone is about to attack and how they may react when you defend yourself. If an assailant's speech is slurred because of alcohol you may, for example, decide that running away may be your best option because people who are drunk cannot run efficiently; or the agitated voice of a junkie puts you on guard against desperate behaviour such as grabbing your mobile phone or necklace. Lying is another form of attack that listening can protect us against - when somebody lies it creates a disharmony within them as the intellectual content of what they are saying does not quite match the emotional expression in their voice or their body language; we often perceive this, but do not trust our hearing sufficiently to believe it.

It is also important to learn how to listen to someone, to perceive the intellectual content and speech patterns contained in their voice, whilst simultaneously sensing their body, in order that you are not 'taken in' by the conversation and miss the vital clues that their body may give out just before an attack. A common ploy by muggers is to approach someone for something simple such as the time or directions and then initiate their attack while the victim is mentally engaged in responding to the question. You should train the perception of body language to override all other processes so that if your awareness perceives a punch coming towards you this impression overrides, for example, thinking about what time it is.

Developing your hearing also allows you to not be suckered into a fight or situation because someone has taunted you. Recall a time when someone insulted you in a particularly painful way, and how the anger rose through your body at lightning speed and a vitriolic response came flying out of your mouth as your body simultaneously contorted into an aggressive shape! This we can classify as a Yang reaction. The opposite Yin reaction is equally as dangerous as in this case an aggressor's taunt causes a reaction but you keep it 'bottled up' inside where it burns away for days, weeks, months, sometimes even lifetimes. This is quite common in relationships where one partner is continually putting down the other – over the course of years this can result in mental and physical illness and total loss of self-esteem. Your hearing in this case can help to identify the recurring themes in your partner's insults thereby making you more prepared to use your presence to ground the energy from the reaction, and from there to gradually find ways of repelling the attack.

All of the examples we have looked at in this section work by developing an awareness, through being present, to the exact moment when your ears receive a shocking impression. This creates a 'gap' in between the reception of the impression and your body's reaction to it, allowing you to redirect some of the energy before it takes the body by surprise. This redirection cannot take place by listening alone but joins up with your Meditation skills, for instance, centring the body to create a powerful line of defence that weakens the shock that an assailant's perceived strike will cause in your body.

We mentioned earlier that one of the biggest obstacles to building a direct harmonious connection with your body is internal conversation. This obstacle has been recognized by many of the great systems of human evolution – Buddhists, for instance, sometimes call it 'monkey chatter'. Developing your hearing can help you to become more sensitive to its operation inside you, particularly to habitual thought patterns. If you take a moment to think about it I am sure you can identify some recurring thoughts that you use to attack yourself with; these can be fairly trivial thoughts such as 'my bum's too big', or more serious thoughts such as 'I'm a loser'. These habitual thoughts uttered over and over again in your mind become like mantras (the word 'mantra' actually means 'seed thought') and very subtly change your behaviour, which people around you will begin to notice. In this way, internal conversation can rob you of many opportunities for growth, but by becoming increasingly aware of it you will gradually become convinced of the necessity to free yourself from its effects.

Over the years, my schooling in music, Meditation and Martial Art has introduced me to various exercises for the development of listening, such is the importance that they all placed on it. The exercises for Outer Meditation – for hearing, touch and sight – all need to be done whilst keeping contact, as much as possible, with the areas of Inner Meditation. The aim of Outer Meditation is to develop peripheral awareness in all three of these senses and then gradually blend them into one 'seamless web of awareness'.

The Exercise for Hearing

1 *Following directly on from the Harmonizing the Body exercise, gradually direct your attention to the sensation of your ears.*
2 *Expand your listening to encompass a 360-degree radius around you.*
3 *Open to the sounds that reach your ears but try not to label them individually (for instance, as a car or somebody talking) and instead listen to everything as if it was a strange kind of music.*
4 *After you have searched your 360-degree radius for sounds, pinpoint one particular sound and focus on it. Relax and try to experience the sound as a vibration travelling through the medium of the air and impacting upon your eardrums.*
5 *After you have stayed with the sound for a while, stay focused on it but open your hearing to listen to all the sounds available to you.*
6 *Strengthen your connection internally with your feet and the breath.*
7 *When you feel you can hold these connections together shift your focus point to another sound within the 360-degree radius.*

This exercise should follow on directly from Inner Meditation and strengthens your awareness of the radius immediately around you. Not 'labelling' the sound allows you to listen in more detail and experience each sound as a vibration; this is good practice for analysing an assailant's speech patterns or footsteps. Utilizing a focus point (a specific sound) at the same time as listening to the 360-degree radius (nonspecific) helps to orientate you in the three-dimensional space and pinpoint a potential danger. Connecting to the feet and breath whilst listening helps to ground any violent reaction in the body due to a sound, for instance, when somebody screams directly at us.

the sense of touch

The skin is the body's largest sense organ and forms the sensitive porous membrane that protects you from viruses and infection and receives impressions from the environment such as temperature and air pressure. The information received through the skin allows your body to keep itself in a state of homeostasis with the external environment. Through the medium of physical pain, it also alerts us to areas of the body that need our attention. The skin works in close association with both the somatic and autonomic nervous systems, for example, if you feel an object with your eyes closed you can still identify it through touch (somatic) or if the air temperature rises you begin to sweat (autonomic).

Because of the skin's sensitivity and its close relationship with our nervous system, the evolution of the sense of touch plays a large part in authentic training in Martial Art. This awareness increases your ability to judge someone's distance from you, which is an indispensable skill when dealing with invasion of personal space, one of the most common forms of aggression in the workplace. Moreover, it develops your ability to use the Strategy of Distance. *(see page 181)* Equally important, this sense allows you to develop what is known as a contact reflex. Anyone who has truly experienced a street fight knows that it happens at the speed of reflex action and not at the speed of thought. Through correct training it is possible to learn reflexive responses to any particular attack, thus bypassing the need for conscious thought to initiate your technique *(see Strategy of Pressure, page 207)*. Conscious thought always uses the process of 'recognition and naming', in other words it must first recognize the body mechanics of a strike before it accesses the memory to find a corresponding technique. But, like your hand pulling away from a flame when it gets too near, a reflex action automatically initiates the correct technique, allowing you to avoid the more complicated processes of conscious thought.

The best preparation for the development of a contact reflex is to build the pathways to the skin. The process for this is outlined in the exercise for touch later. Conflict situations usually always involve some kind of touch between your body and the assailant's and, whether somebody grabs, pushes or punches you, the sensations enter the body via the skin. These sensations can tell you a great deal about a person – they can communicate to the brain beyond the level of conscious thought. For instance, a good hypnotist will use a subtle touch to cue a person into a hypnotic state. Similarly, a good pickpocket may use the sensations of bumping into you to disguise the more subtle sensations of him reaching into your pocket. The process of Meditation develops an overall body awareness (as outlined in peripheral awareness earlier, *see page 105*) as an essential part of self-defence. The sense of touch plays a large role in this by preventing our awareness from getting 'fixed' in one place, For example, when an assailant grabs an untrained person they will respond to the grab by directing most of their attention to the point where they have been grabbed. They will then try to wrestle their assailant's hands from the grab's point of contact, which is actually the most difficult place to free yourself from. Your attention is drawn to this point because the body perceives it as the most dangerous point *(see the first Chi Kung exercise, page 151)* and then the attention becomes fixed here, which stops you from using the vast power of your overall body mechanics to break the grip. The sense of touch allows us to combat this tendency to focus on one place and instead spread the attention over the whole body, allowing us to 'ground' the sensations of panic that often accompany being grabbed and find an efficient technique for dealing with the situation.

At a more subtle level, when somebody moves towards you it creates a change in the air pressure around your body. If it is a Yang movement (expanding), such as a punch, that is coming towards you, the air is compressed; if it is a Yin movement (contracting) and they draw away from you, then a vacuum is created and the air is pulled away from you. Both these movements can be sensed and can trigger an appropriate response. One of the practices in traditional Martial Art training that develops the sensitivity to this level is blindfold sparring. Here, the use of the blindfold removes the visual channel and forces the sense of touch to develop in order to fill the space left by the absent sight. By training in this way it is possible to tell from the touch of somebody's arm where their feet are placed, how tall they are, how dense their muscles are, how emotionally agitated they are, what they are thinking of doing next, and so on. It is like putting a 'bugging' device on someone and listening to what is going on inside them. When you have this kind of awareness it is very difficult for an opponent to make any movement without it being 'telegraphed' through their arms or any other part of their body that you may be touching. This creates a direct link to your trained reflexes so that they can be triggered easily from somebody's movement. Once again, this happens at a speed that our normal conscious mind cannot follow, thus the mind must be trained to find its correct place in relation to movement, that is taking a 'backseat' and only monitoring rather than directing the movement.

Like with the sense of hearing, bringing awareness to the sense of touch creates a 'gap' between an impression as it impacts upon your skin and the reaction inside your body. This distance gives you the ability to immediately ground a significant portion of the impression's energy so that shock cannot gain as powerful a hold on the body when the brain perceives the threat. Not only does this significantly increase our ability to 'perform' under pressure, but also from here we can take the first steps towards the control of pain. Pain travelling through your body takes a certain amount of bioelectricity, but if you have gained a degree of control over the movement of this energy it is possible to direct it away from the pain's point of origin, thereby decreasing its effects. This principle could similarly be used for the control of emotional pain. For example, if you think back to a time where you experienced emotional pain – perhaps on splitting up with a partner – the memory of that pain is likely to return like an echo. But by developing connections to your body through the practice of Meditation you will subtly learn how to redirect your energy and gently pull it away from these memories. Thus you start to work with the process of homeostasis by at first becoming aware of these areas of pain and then releasing and letting them go. In this way, working through the physical body allows you to communicate with your emotional self, which is very often trapped in a somewhat immature state when it comes to dealing with pain or emotional wounds. This kind of work bears many fruits for the self, not least of which is the tremendous saving of energy that occurs when you

 The Intelligent Warrior

stop torturing yourself with various memories and apprehensions.

Your senses of hearing and touch work closely together in a similar way to your senses of taste and smell. Your body actually receives many sounds through the skin – anyone who has stood near a loud bass speaker at a nightclub will have a real impression of this, and the effects of powerful sound waves on the body can be far-reaching. There was a French scientist in the 19th century who studied the harmonic patterns of the French police whistle. To do so he built himself a 6-foot version of the whistle and manipulated it with compressed air, using a devised control room with a wall between him and the whistle. On his first testing he accidentally let the whistle ring and his assistant, who was still in the room with the whistle, was killed by the sound rupturing his internal organs. Although less intense than this, life in a busy city surrounds us with a variety of violent sounds, many of a mechanical nature, and this causes the body to feel attacked and so protect itself by creating armour in the form of tension. This tension can be violent such as after being surprised by a car backfiring, or quite subtle such as the continual roar of traffic outside the window, and creates an underlying level of tension that facilitates what we know as stress. The practice of Meditation opens you to the sensations coming from the skin and builds a strong enough communication with the flow of energy in the body to redirect the energy away from the muscular tension. The third dimension of the Centring the Body exercise *(see page 56)* is the key practice for releasing muscular tension, and in that exercise we familiarize ourselves with the two fundamental directions of energy in the body: upwards with increasing tension and downwards with the command of 'release'.

The Exercise for Touch

1 *Following directly on from the exercise for hearing, turn your attention to any impression that is flowing in from the skin such as the sensation of clothing, shoes, jewellery or air temperature.*

2 *Find a focus point, such as the sensation of your left shoe, and try to receive a more detailed impression of it.*

3 *Hold this focus point and return to your overall sensation from the skin.*

4 *Reconnect with the Tan T'ien and skeletal alignment.*

5 *When you feel you can hold these connections shift your focus point to another sensation, perhaps the sensation of your collar.*

This exercise is an excellent preparation for applying armlocks and wristlocks or their counters as there is always a tendency for our attention to be taken to the point of the grab. Holding your attention over the whole body and connecting to the Tan T'ien and skeleton allows you to apply body mechanics to breaking or applying a hold. This exercise also prepares the way for training utilizing the Strategy of Pressure *(see page 207)*.

the sense of sight

Don't feel disappointed; it takes a long time to
train the eyes properly.   Castaneda (1972: 68)

We depend on our sense of sight more than on any of the other
senses and this is largely due to our Western education with its
overemphasis on reading and writing. Ever since we learned how
to read, we have been bombarding our minds with all kinds of
facts, philosophies and notions. Advertising, newspapers, books
and language all play a part in this overloading of the sight. The
physiology of the eyes also presupposes us to connect more with
the intellectual functions; the effect of this has been to drag us
into a very one-dimensional or literal view of the world where we
perceive the surface of things much more than their true nature.
Jacques Lusseyran writes:

> It is often said that seeing brings us closer to
> things. Seeing certainly permits orientation, the
> possibility of finding our way in space. But with
> what part of an object does that acquaint us? It
> establishes a relationship with the surface of

This tendency to perceive the surface of things is very dangerous in self-defence; we must train our sight to perceive the subtle clues that a situation or a potential attacker will give off, which will warn us of danger at an early stage. We must not be taken in by first appearances but train the eyes to perceive a potential danger, such as a dark street or an approaching body, with a deeper insight.

You have at your disposal two kinds of sight: specific sight, which most people tend to use all of the time, and nonspecific sight, which offers a new possibility of seeing. Specific sight focuses on one thing at a time and generally flits unconsciously from one thing to another. From the moment you got up this morning your eyes will have been focusing and refocusing on various objects such as your alarm clock, door handle, hallway, bathroom door, toilet, and so on. Nonspecific sight has the ability to view the whole picture; it utilizes peripheral awareness, where everything in the field of vision is seen equally. To experience nonspecific sight try this: pick a point in front of you and stare at it (a point about 15 feet away from you is best), and as you do this open up your peripheral awareness 90 degrees to the sides (so that you can see the walls of the room perhaps) and 90 degrees up and down (floor and ceiling). Our specific sight fixes at one point whereas our nonspecific sight expands to take in the whole field of vision. Some theorists believe that we have evolved these two kinds of sight by having to look at horizons (nonspecific) whilst also pinpointing prey (specific). The utilization of the sight in this way is one of your greatest tools for self-defence.

The focus for specific sight I will call a 'focus point'. Your ability to discipline the eyes to hold a focus point, first in the relaxed situation of Meditation then, gradually, into increasingly random situations, is one of the keys to *presence* and *awareness*. One of the most common reactions when the body goes into shock is for the eyes to lose their ability to focus on any one thing and so they violently flit from one thing to another. A tactic used by ambulance attendants and other emergency personnel when faced with someone in shock is to look them in the eyes and say, 'look at me, look at me' whilst pointing to their eyes. Anchoring the person's attention on something that is not moving has the effect of bringing the person back into reality. The popular sayings 'they lost their head' or 'fell to pieces' hint at the tendency for inner disintegration in the body. By developing the ability to focus steadily on one point we gain a powerful tool to keep us grounded and together in a stressful situation; it also provides a centre for our nonspecific sight to expand from. To understand how this can be applied directly to self-defence we will look at the following example: whilst walking at night you suddenly become *aware* that ahead of you the road is not very well lit. You select something ahead of you, such as a traffic sign, and use it as your focus point and simultaneously begin to 'open up' your nonspecific sight. Just using the sight in this way will subtly change how your body will be perceived by a potential assailant as you will walk straighter and with more purpose and will give off the 'air' of somebody who has power and knows where they are going. As mentioned previously, muggers are looking for people who are 'not there' and daydreaming. This means that they can approach without their victim ever knowing and therefore gain the maximum shock value from their attack, hoping to 'freeze' their victim with the energy from fight-or-flight response so that they can then take what they want. If you are present and walking with purpose a mugger will think twice about attacking you. However, if they do try to approach then your nonspecific sight will alert you to their presence at the earliest opportunity, which will allow you to prepare for a direct confrontation. In this situation, your focus point would now move to between your attacker's eyes, just below the eyebrows. A focus point will help stop the mind from panicking, and by holding our eyes steady our nonspecific sight can then watch the totality of the attacker's body for clues as to their intentions. In addition, if you decide to run you can watch out of the 'corner of your eye' for a definite direction to run in, such as a lit street, without alerting your attacker to your intentions. We will look into situations like this in more depth in the Martial Art section.

The development of your focus point can be a valuable asset whenever you need to emphasize your point of view. Whether in a business meeting or to your partner, there are times when you need to look someone in the eyes and tell them 'what's what', and having developed a steady gaze through Meditation will increase the likelihood of you being able to use it in such situations.

The development of nonspecific sight teaches your brain to work in a new way. It allows you to perceive a relationship between objects in the visual field, for instance, the biomechanical relationship between the hands and feet when someone is striking you. This is comparable to an artist who learns how to see the 'whole' so they can perceive the relationship of various shapes, forms, and shades of colour in their painting; or to a good architect who learns to look at the whole building in terms of the proportions of its various components. In order to utilize the sense of sight efficiently and develop a true 'insight' to see past the surface of things in the disturbing situation of a conflict, the Intelligent Warrior needs to find a balance between specific sight (Yang) and nonspecific sight (Yin) through the practice of Meditation.

The Exercise for Sight

1 *Gently open your eyes and immediately find a focus point. It can be anything directly in front of you but it must be stationary and approximately at eye level.*
2 *Expand your peripheral awareness 90 degrees on each side (you should be able to see both walls if you are in a rectangular room) and 90 degrees up and down (to the floor and ceiling).*
3 *Reconnect with your five points of coordination and your feet on the ground.*

The sight is the most distracting of all the senses because it is so closely connected to our intellectual functions; it also tends to be the one sense more than any other that we depend on habitually. Finding a focus point immediately stops the eyes from flitting from one thing to another which would have the tendency to generate internal conversation. It also helps you to develop a steady gaze, which is an indispensable part of your presence. Opening up your peripheral awareness allows you to scan a larger area in one go, and this is helpful if you are talking directly to an assailant but perhaps need to look for a way out at the same time. It is also excellent preparation for learning how to read another person's body mechanics.

the seamless web
of awareness

The senses would continue to exist, because
their role as natural intermediaries has been
established by the order of creation itself. But they
would no longer work independently, separated
from each other, as we have wrongly assumed they
must. From just this 'total attention' the seeing are
constantly diverted. So are the blind, but not to the
same degree. For them remaining attentive is a
practical necessity, and this simple fact constitutes
the first of their gifts.

Hearing, sense of smell, sense of touch! Truly i
hesitate to make these differences because i am
afraid they are arbitrary.

Lusseyran (1999: 59)

We have now studied Meditation in some detail. We have looked at
each individual aspect, learned why each aspect is necessary and
have the tools, in the form of exercises, to develop each one. Each
aspect provides you with a particular skill that brings more

authenticity to your self-defence practice. Without Meditation it is difficult for holistic self-defence to work in your life and, as we said earlier, for it to channel the incredible power of the reaction of the fight-or-flight response. If we continue to work on developing each of these areas, something extraordinary will begin to happen – they begin to merge into one awareness. This is what you are aiming to build; a heightened state of awareness characterized by a relaxed body brought together with a very active and aware 'inner life'. This state is both your first and second line of defence: awareness and presence are your most powerful tools for defending your homeostasis. Gradually, as these different aspects of the Meditation process are sensed as one, you will have an inner awareness (or Yin), comprising of the centre, alignment definition and harmonization of the body, and an outer awareness, comprising our three main senses in a state of peripheral awareness. A silence in the mind, a relaxation in the body and a stillness in the emotions characterize this overall state of awareness when felt as a whole. It is the sensation of your body, mind and spirit coming into balance. This state is what some American Indians described in their warrior training as a 'seamless web of awareness'.

To understand this further we may look at two analogies: the first is a spider's web from the American Indian tradition; and the second is from Buddhism and likens awareness to a placid lake. The idea of the spider web is useful because it gives us a certain perspective on the whole. A spider sits at the centre of its web from where the web spreads out in a 360-degree radius. The web also has a certain dynamic tension – not too loose, not too tight. As the prey lands it creates a vibration that flows down the web and reaches the spider, making the spider aware of its prey. Here you can see the role of a stable centre, the expanding of the awareness (the web) out from the centre, and the reception of vibration. No doubt the spider can also tell the size and aliveness of its prey through the vibration as well. So, vibration communicates more than just the presence but also certain qualities of its prey. The second analogy compares the primary qualities of our awareness – stillness and balance – to a calm body of water. This body of water has a certain surface tension to it so if a pebble is thrown into the water it creates ripples that emanate outwards in a waveform (vibration), 'washing-up' on anything in the way. So if we take this analogy of ourselves as the calm lake, then the surface tension of the water is like the spider's web and our opponent is the pebble which creates a vibration that can be sensed. These analogies are more useful than an intellectual description because they allow us to 'feel' this principle in an energetic format.

The seamless web of awareness is an energetic state that we build very carefully. First the components are inner and outer parts, then gradually as these separate parts evolve they begin to meld into one. The strength of this state is measured by its ability to withstand shock, such as when somebody screams at you. It is not a rigid state but one of flexibility and impeccable balance. The more you work on it and bring it into your life, the more it becomes a versatile tool for all the various forms of conflict that you may find in the battlefield of your life.

The Exercise for the Seamless Web of Awareness

After you have gone through the whole process of Inner and Outer Meditation, try to bring an overall awareness together using the following exercise:

1 Open to the sensations from your inner and outer 'worlds' simultaneously. Do not worry if you can only keep contact with a few areas to start with.

2 Decide on a number of breaths (five is good to start with), and gently connect to your breathing counting each breath backwards, for instance, from five to one.

3 As you do this, do not allow your body to make even the slightest movement, apart from blinking and breathing. However, do not hold it still rigidly with muscular tension but relax and try to find a point of stillness. Resist the temptation to fidget or enter into its mental equivalent – internal conversation.

4 Relax as you breathe and try to open and include more and more impressions in your awareness.

5 Try to allow a relaxation in the body, quietness in the mind and stillness in the emotions to infuse your being.

This exercise develops a total state of awareness that, if practised, you can instantaneously turn to at any time in your life. Keeping the body still increases your awareness to anything that moves within its 'web'. When you get more adept at creating this state of awareness, try to increase the number of breaths that you remain in it. When you feel it is time to stop, gently rise up out of the stance, breathing out simultaneously through the nose, and then consciously decide to leave the state and return to your 'normal' life.

HOW TO PRACTiCE THE PROCESS OF MEDiTATiON

Finding time in your life to practice Meditation can sometimes be a problem, and you will probably have to fight to make a space in your schedule for it. Here are some tips on how to achieve this.

1   *Apply the 'little and often' rule. It is much better to practice in short amounts frequently than it is to practice for long periods infrequently. This ensures a regular input of energy in the form of time spent paying attention to the conscious repetition (see page 149) of the process. It is much better to practice for five minutes a day for seven days in a row than to practice 35 minutes just once a week.*

2   *Try to practice in the morning. When you get up in the morning your habitual energy circuits have not fully woken up. There is a greater opportunity for you to forge new circuits before all your habitual movements, thoughts and emotional states begin to 'kick in' and take all of your energy. In addition, the oxygen in the atmosphere is at its most nourishing (and less polluted) early in the morning.*

3   *In your practice sessions, always try to go through the whole process. Even if you condense it down into the time it takes your kettle to boil, try to touch all the areas of Meditation. Follow the guide below in order to get a feel for the whole process.*

4   *Find moments during your day when you can 'touch' an aspect of your Meditation techniques. This is crucial for your practice to have meaning in your life, which we will deal with at length in the Martial Art section. Briefly, there are many times during your day where you can practice Meditation, such as whilst waiting for a bus or walking to work. At these times we can reconnect with our meditative state by perhaps connecting to the alignment of the*

spine. In so doing we can transform any situation we may find ourselves in into profitable 'time spent'.

5   Be wary of internal conversation. When it comes to avoiding work or practising a skill there is no end to the creativity of our internal conversation for making excuses. Everyone *can find some time* in their day to practice, even if it is only for a couple of minutes.

The following is a summary of the sequence of Meditation:

1   Stand in the Basic Stance with your eyes closed.
2   Centre the Body: connect to the Tan T'ien via the three dimensions of the centre.
3   Align the Body: connect to the triangular base, spine and head. Go from the feet to the head, and then from the head to the feet. This practice maintains biomechanical health (Body).
4   Define the Body: connect to the five points of coordination. This practice maintains bioelectrical health (Mind).
5   Harmonize the Body: connect to the Natural Breath Cycle. This practice maintains biochemical health (Spirit).
6   The Hearing: connect to your hearing and utilize peripheral awareness. Be sure to maintain connection to Inner Meditation.
7   The Touch: open to the sensations coming in from the skin.
8   The Sight: open the eyes and find a focus point immediately.
9   The Seamless Web of Awareness: open to all impressions, inner and outer.

This sequence can be done in as little as two minutes but you should be aiming to take about 15 minutes. Try to always go through the whole process.

PART TWO

CHi KUNG

introduction

Chi Kung is a form of exercise dating from around 2500 BC that has been evolved by many practitioners over the years and is used all over the world today. As with a lot of Chinese disciplines, it is difficult to get an accurate picture of where and how Chi Kung first originated. I am not going to try and answer these question in any great depth as there are many books available on the subject; however, there are some features in its development that are significant for our study.

The term 'Chi Kung' roughly translated means 'breath work' or 'breath power'. It involves strengthening the mechanics of correct breathing and harmonizing the breath with complimentary movements to enhance the Natural Breath Cycle *(see page 95)*. Traditionally it has played a huge part in the development of Chinese medicine and Martial Art practices.

Central to the understanding of Chi Kung is the concept of Chi, which the Chinese describe as the vital energy of a human being, and which is largely extracted from the air during the process of breathing but is then balanced with the energy from physical food and the food of impressions. It is a fairly difficult and somewhat futile task to pinpoint exactly what Chi is. There are those in the Martial Art world who, like a blind man denying the existence of colour, ridicule it and say it is a bunch of Chinese hogwash. Others are seduced by quasi-mystical imaginings of what it is and drift off in satin Kung Fu suits. Both of these attitudes are misleading and, like much of our efforts in this book, the concept of Chi can only be understood by opening to a direct experience of it in the body; in other words, we need to build a sensitivity to it. This Chi could then be used for maintaining a healthy state in the body, healing others, spiritual development and self-defence (to 'neutralize' attackers).

Chi Kung plays a vital part in our study of holistic self-defence because it strengthens our health and equilibrium and acts as a bridge between Meditation and actual self-defence techniques. It is, if you like, a moving Meditation because after building a heightened state of awareness in a stationary position we start carefully to try and keep the connection to this state as we move. There are three exercises to be learned which have been pared down and adapted for modern society from some of the original Shaolin exercises and are designed to work specifically in conjunction with the other primary areas of study presented in this book.

HISTORY

One of the difficulties in studying Chinese disciplines is that their history is shrouded in myth and legend, poetic metaphor, mind-bending conundrums and downright deception. For this reason I have never found it a tremendously fruitful endeavour to try and make the origins of particular disciplines crystal clear. However, in the history of Chi Kung there are certain significant events that crop up. For instance, we do know that the practice of Chi Kung is ancient as it features very heavily in *The Yellow Emperor's Classic of Internal Medicine*, the earliest and probably most significant medical work. It is also fairly certain that Chi Kung started life as a spiritual/healing dance in much the same vein as that of African or American Indian traditions; the repeated powerful patterns of movement harmonized with repeated patterns of breath (chanting or singing) to heal or evoke a heightened state of awareness are clear precursors to the early, more formal, Chi Kung exercises. It evolved side by side with Chinese medicine, and along with acupuncture, Chinese massage, herbal medicine and cosmology played a key role in the understanding of Chi in the body. Somewhere along the line it got hijacked for martial purposes – the Chinese have been practising Martial Art since the beginning of their recorded history and as they became healthier through the practice of Chi Kung it started to be used not just for the defence of one's health but also for the more expansionist practices of war. Significant for us is Bodidharma's discovery of the Shaolin temples for it is here we see the birth of modern Chi Kung; its evolution is fairly traceable, although rather shrouded in the myriad styles and practitioners all claiming to be the authentic line. Bodidharma (as you remember from the Introduction) introduced certain exercises to the monks in order to maintain their physical wellbeing while they were engaged in the somewhat intellectual task of transcribing Sanskrit to Chinese. The monks' health soon significantly improved and they started to develop the Chi Kung practices (largely by meditating upon nature) into the early Kung Fu animal forms. It was also at this time that Chi Kung joined forces with Taoist practices (particularly the *I Ching*) and T'ai Chi Ch'uan was born.

Various neighbouring countries, either by mutual proximity or invasion, have been influenced by Chi Kung practices, evolving similar forms of exercise in conjunction with Martial Art and medicine. Today Chi Kung is practised all over the world. Whilst this is of course a good thing, it does unfortunately mean (mainly due to the same process as the party game *Chinese whispers*) that there is an incredible number of styles and variations, the majority with little authentic content. Rather than focusing on the pros and cons of various styles, it is more helpful to examine what good Chi Kung should incorporate.

HEALTH

In Part II, Meditation, the health benefits of correct breathing were described in some detail in the 'Harmonization of the Body' chapter *(see page 55)*. We then went on to find the Natural Breath Cycle in the body. Chi Kung picks up from where this left off and strengthens this Natural Breath Cycle by exercising the biomechanics used in breathing. Chi Kung not only strengthens all the aforementioned health benefits of correct breathing but also brings some additional quite specific health benefits.

In Chi Kung we start to work the diaphragm and associated abdominal muscles more, while trying not to interfere with the length of the Natural Breath Cycle. The breath cycle needs to be strengthened in both directions equally so that the diaphragm can not only push out air with the aid of the abdominal muscles but also pull it down into the lungs with equal power. The Chinese likened the interplay between the diaphragm and abdominal muscles to a set of bellows (the type you would use to get a fire going) – you push the handles together to force the air out, and pull them apart to force the air back in again. By strengthening the breath cycle in this way, the tendency for the breath to return to the Natural Breath Cycle during the day is far greater as the power of the these muscles will remind you to breath correctly. They also massage the intestines with increased force, aiding in digestion and the effective elimination of the body's waste products, and, along with the increased movement of intercostal muscles, keep the whole spine, including the neck and ribcage, supple and allow for greater volumes of air to be taken into the lungs.

One of the biggest benefits of doing Chi Kung correctly is that it increases the flow of air being pulled in through the nose and sinus cavities; this increased airflow dries the sinuses out and brings a correct balance of mucus to the lining of the nose. The vast majority of urban dwellers have sinuses that are clogged up with mucus due to poor breathing habits, air pollution and a high mucus-forming diet. This unhealthy state of the sinus cavities causes headaches, poor balance, tiredness, a susceptibility to viruses, and ear, nose and throat infections. It takes about 150 per cent more effort to breath through the nose than the mouth because of certain functions performed by the nose, including the warming and filtering of incoming air so as not to shock the respiratory system, the monitoring of atmospheric equilibrium, and the efficient removal of negative ion particles through its olfactory nerves. This last function has a lot to do with the development of Chi in the body as the negative ion particles carry a charge vital for our wellbeing. The increased airflow through the nose also helps to balance the pressure coming from each nostril into the sinuses, which strengthens the inside of the nose, making the olfactory nerves work more efficiently and stopping the tiny blood vessels in the nose from bursting as a result of blowing your nose, heightened aerobic activity or a change in atmospheric pressure. In addition, harmonizing the breath with movements increases blood circulation, while the rhythmic nature of the movements helps to pump the blood into the extremities which, coupled with the increase of oxygen in the blood, allows unused capillaries in the body to open up and be nourished. This fact alone greatly increases your general state of wellbeing for it allows a deeper communication and equilibrium to be set up in the body.

In the Meditation section we went to some trouble to align the skeleton correctly *(see page 69)*. The movements in Chi Kung strengthen this alignment by a gravitational pulse that is set up through the body via the rhythmic movement of the arms. As the arms move they pull on the skeleton and, if our alignment is strong, the central core is not pulled off balance and the pull is channelled down through the legs into the ground. The effect of this is that the spine is gently pulled into a stronger position of alignment. The pulse into the ground also strengthens the relationship between the tendons, ligaments, bones and muscles in the legs that protect the skeleton, much like shock absorbers in a car, against the impact of the foot hitting the ground, especially in times of powerful movement. Chi Kung also introduces circular movements into the joints of the arms, which are extremely important movements in Chi Kung. Three circular movements are available to us, located at the wrist, elbow and shoulder joints, and rotating these joints helps to free the movement of Chi to the hands. In Western society it is rare to regularly make rotational movements with the joints, yet opening them up keeps them supple, free from toxins and well lubricated. Chi Kung strengthens the energy meridians that run like a wiring system through the body. Because the movements are rhythmic and repeated the same neural messages travel down from the cerebellum to the various parts of the body, and set up an energy pulse that gradually unblocks the movement of energy in the meridians. An acupuncturist would stimulate these same meridians with a needle.

Once learned, Chi Kung can be practised well into old age; it does not destroy the body as jogging, weightlifting and other sports do, but on the contrary rejuvenates and keeps the body flexible, which is vital in old age.

This is by no means an exhaustive list of the health benefits of practising Chi Kung but it serves as a guide to the type of advantages you can expect to gain. Many books delve deeper into the subject but you must be careful because some can be hopelessly convoluted and this is a luxury you cannot afford in self-defence.

Shaping the Body of Attention

As mentioned earlier, Chi Kung forms a bridge between Meditation and technique (Martial Science) so when looking at the self-defence benefits of practising it we could divide it into those categories. In the process of Meditation our first movement was to centre our bodies and then gradually move outwards through the skeleton, muscles and skin until we were relating, via the senses, to the world outside us, while still keeping an inner connection to the centre. We now move one more step away from the centre by starting to physically move the body; this makes the connection with the centre and other areas of Meditation even more difficult. However, if we can slowly build a connection between the breath and the movements then our presence will become more fluid and our body, mind and spirit will be able to perform daily tasks and self-defence techniques with more integration. Each of the three Chi Kung exercises strengthens movement in one of the three spatial dimensions: the first moves the hands from left to right; the second, forwards and back; and the third, up and down. Every movement you make is made up of these three directions and it is in this way that we strengthen not only the physical movements themselves but also the impulse from the body of attention to make the physical movement.

In the Definition of the Body chapter in the Meditation section we brought the body of attention into the physical body so that it took on the same shape as the physical body. Now we begin to change the shape of the body of attention, which in turn allows us to move the physical body into that shape. This is significant because we are beginning to feel the movements before physically manifesting them, and this sensing from the inside strengthens our ability to move when under pressure. Additionally, we are harmonizing these movements in the three spatial dimensions with an exact pattern of breath. This connection means that if we make a movement physically it will remind the breath to 'kick in' and start the correct breath technique; conversely, if in times of conflict we remember to breathe correctly, our movements become free. One of the effects of the energy travelling upwards in the body when we are afraid is the 'freezing' of the breath, which usually follows a sharp intake. This tends to freeze our movements or at best makes them very stiff causing the execution of a technique or gesture, no matter how well practised, to become severely debilitated.

The practice of Chi Kung builds the underlying structure of all movement, but especially self-defence techniques. The harmonization that occurs in their repeated patterns teaches the body which movements are Yang (expanding) and which are Yin (contracting), bringing a much deeper understanding of self-defence techniques. Every movement you make works on this Yin/Yang pattern; for instance, a Yang movement might be your hand moving away from the body to strike whilst the Yin movement might be the hand drawing back to you, perhaps changing its shape. The Yang movements tend to be made on the 'out' breath, whereas Yin movements are usually made on the 'in' breath. With movements that are more complex, various very subtle relationships exist between the physical movement and breath. An Intelligent Warrior should acquire an in-depth knowledge of the Yin/Yang phases of movement.

Each of the three Chi Kung moves also inhibits a certain tendency or reaction that the body initiates when it loses its centre. For example, the Movement of the Chi exercise works against the body's tendency to always orientate itself around the point it perceives as the most dangerous, such as when the body immediately reacts to a punch thrown at its head by turning towards the punch, pulling the head back and throwing an arm up towards it *(see Photograph 9)*. This hard-wired response has been programmed by nature as a basic self-defence reaction, and unfortunately it tends to override everything else, including carefully rehearsed techniques. To fully understand this we need to cross-reference it with the exercise itself and an actual self-defence technique. The photographs are representations of the body mechanics and not exact interpretations of fight scenarios.

9

10

11

In the first Chi Kung exercise we are training the ability to respond to a punch without losing our centre or the focus point that rests upon the central core of our opponent *(see Twist Punch page 196)*. The second exercise (forwards and back) combats the tendency in the human body to apply force from the head. This tendency makes us lean forwards from the upper body when we strike and causes tunnel vision (a narrowing of the field of vision onto the target as we strike; *see assailant on the left in Photograph 10)*. The third exercise (up and down) works against the tendency for energy to rise in times of stress *(see Photograph 11)*, which we have already discussed at some length.

We will delve a little deeper into these reactions later, but it is important here to note that these tendencies also affect us in our lives in many more subtle ways because of their deep subconscious origins. For example, we can see the first tendency manifest when we have a pressing problem or fear and we find it difficult to concentrate as our mind is always being pulled back (orientating itself) to the problem. The second tendency is apparent when we try to solve the problem through 'racking our brains' (applying force from the head), which hampers the mind's ability to think creatively or laterally. I have lost count of the number of scientists and artists alike who have told me that their best ideas originated whilst walking, in the bath or on the toilet; all activities that pull you out of your head and into your physical body. The third tendency presents itself when pressure from the problem or fear increases such as whilst waiting for the results of medical tests; as the time for receiving the results approaches, the fear (energy) begins to rise proportionally upwards in your body, often exacerbating the symptoms of your medical problem. Through conscious repetition *(see page 111)* the Intelligent Warrior sees that the mind and body are inextricably linked, and that by strengthening the body against the three tendencies the mind (intent) and spirit are strengthened through the Principle of Resonation.

Strengthening the breath cycle via Chi Kung also ensures a continued balance between 'in' and 'out' breaths so that in times of extreme exertion we maintain our Chi levels. Depletion of Chi is one of the major factors in a street confrontation. Although the physical fitness one attains from sport is quite advantageous, the nature of a street fight causes such a massive reaction in the body that it tends to eradicate any advantage of being physically fit. A long-distance runner has great stamina, but only in their particular 'running state' where they are relaxed and not bothered by people trying to hit them; on the other hand, someone who has grown up in a tough neighbourhood and received violence since an early age, even if they smoke and drink like a trooper, will outlast a very fit person who has little experience of violence. When the body goes into shock it burns Chi rapidly without any provision for replacing it (hyperventilation is a desperate attempt by the body to regain its homeostasis when in shock), but the practice of Meditation lessens the effect of shock through awareness and presence, and Chi Kung develops the ability for the body to replenish itself quickly and efficiently in times of stress. If your Chi becomes depleted then your body will begin a process to protect itself by drawing your energy away from the extremities first (you will not be able to lift your arm or leg). It will then take away your upright structure to save energy (you will fall to the ground), and unconsciousness will soon follow. If depletion continues afterwards, then cardiac arrest may occur. One of my most frustrating moments occurred during a fairly protracted street fight where I eventually manoeuvred my opponent into a position where I could deliver a knee to his head (he was bent over and my hand had grabbed his hair). Much to my disappointment and shock I found that I could not even raise my leg to perform the technique;

my mind wished to do it but my body did not respond. On reflection I realized that even though this was partly due to being 'out of breath', it was also because the message from my brain to my leg did not have enough energy (Chi) to make the connection (this is the same energy that a stage hypnotist would disrupt in order to stop their subject lifting an arm). Luckily, my opponent was in the same state and so there was a rather comical moment where we were both trying to attack each other but could not move, during which time my body reminded me that my breath cycle was nonexistent. This awareness initiated the correct Chi Kung breathing and, after a couple of breaths, I had the power to sidekick him over a nearby desk. This kind of tiredness tends to be present when any form of anxiety assails the body, so practising Chi Kung is highly recommended for anyone whose professional life puts them at risk, such as emergency-service personnel, doctors and nurses, police, gangsters, soldiers, badly behaved pop stars, and so on.

Through Meditation we develop a stable presence, including a strong vertical alignment. The Chi Kung exercises allow the hands to move freely yet in relation to this stable alignment, without interfering with its balance. The stable core is essential for maintaining uprightness and an accurate sense of distance; however, the hands and arms need to change shape at a much greater frequency in order to deal with the limbs of a constantly shifting opponent.

I will expand on some of these points when we look at the Chi Kung exercises later. The exercises themselves work by repetitive cycles and have been honed over many years into their essential components. Again, the reason for this is simplicity, one of the most essential factors for holistic self-defence.

the process of embodiment

Learn the rules, embody the rules, break the rules.

At first punch was just a punch and the kick was just a kick then punch was not punch and the kick was not the kick and now a punch is just punch and the kick is just a kick.   **Bruce Lee**

A warrior seeks freedom by gently embracing his desire, using it to motivate his mind, so that his mind will instruct the body and the body educate his feeling, enabling his feeling to become his original desire. By the walking in circles he realises his true nature.   **Master Sun Li**

Before attempting to learn the Chi Kung exercises (especially via photographs and words), it would be prudent to outline the process used for learning any new movements.

The process of embodiment is the means by which we take new skills, techniques or ideas from the outside world and internalize and make them part of ourselves. This science was evolved in the early Kung Fu schools where the monks meditated whilst watching animals move, then embodied the essence of these movements and created the original animal forms. The process was then applied to other skills such as music, calligraphy and weaponry. Its basic tenets have survived to this day and have also been rediscovered in the training of many contemporary practices: music, dance and sport training; it also plays a significant part in various therapies such as the Alexander Technique and Neurolinguistic Programming (NLP). Whether you like it or not you are subject to the process of embodiment, and it is up to you how well you wish to play the game or how much you wish to participate in it.

When we embark on a new path of knowledge we start with a wish, perhaps to learn to play a musical instrument, to paint, to drive a car or to learn self-defence. This wish leads us to take some kind of action that we had not taken before, such as gathering information on a subject, purchasing some of the necessary equipment, or seeking out an appropriate teacher. For the most part, such actions are outside of us and information is passed from the outside and assimilated, via our senses, into various parts of our mind. The next step is to try to reproduce the act or skill that you wish to acquire repeatedly over a period of time, because in this way we train the body's nerves and structures in the performance of the task. Patience and perseverance will lead to a certain degree of mastery plus the ability to express ourselves using that skill in the outside world, so completing the cycle making our wish a reality.

Embodying something is an exact method that cannot be short-circuited, circumvented or hurried, and we can save ourselves a lot of time, pain and pulling out of the hair if we study how it operates practically. The common experience of learning to drive can be used as an example. When you first get into a car everything is new to you and, although you may have an idea of what each instrument controls, you have never actually used them; you are also not overly familiar with the road laws that must be obeyed in order to interact safely with other vehicles on the highways which, depending on where you live, could be described as the battlefield! You first must gather information by acquiring the services of a good driving instructor and buying the *Highway Code*; that done, you begin instructing the mind, which in turn instructs the body, thereby gaining experience. The first part of this process is very much a task for your head, for instance, you are instructed to push in the clutch, release the handbrake, put the car in gear, look over your shoulder before moving on, and so on, one instruction follows another as the mind directs the attention to these various tasks. Inevitably our first efforts are awkward, the car lurches forwards, we forget to release the handbrake or to signal, our steering is erratic and we have to start far away from any moving or stationary objects so as to protect them from our inability. This phase is what Bruce Lee called 'learn the rules'. If you are attentive you will see that the mind is quite slow at doing things that involve moving, even though it knows what to do it cannot perform the tasks quickly enough to make a smooth transition from inability to ability immediately. You have to practise – through conscious repetition – your gear changes, signals and so on until they become 'second nature'. At this point the process begins to pass into a new phase called 'embody the rules', which activates the intelligence of the body, rather than the mind, to take control of the necessary movements that have been practised. Your control over the car is no longer incompetent, gear changes and steering are smoother, yet, strangely enough, you do not need to think consciously as much about their execution as before. The mind has taken a back seat and now monitors the movements rather than instructs them directly. You can even hold a conversation while driving, a sure sign that the intellectual functions have become free! The part of the brain that is now primarily controlling the movements is the cerebellum. You can now drive carefully on the roads but have little experience of driving. After you pass your test and regularly drive the roads (more repetition), driving will quickly become completely automatic, and at this point you will begin to feel the act of driving and to express yourself by speeding up, cutting corners and weaving in between traffic without a thought to the thousands upon thousands of computations that your brain/body is making to keep you safe. This phase is called 'breaking the rules'. It does not mean that you literally break the rules of the road, but that you have embodied the skills of driving to such a degree that you can start to 'bend' them without even thinking about it.

This process can be applied to the learning of absolutely anything. I was first introduced to it whilst studying classical guitar. I was first taught how to put my fingers on the guitar then learned about chord shapes etc. This was followed by much practice and repetition, until I reached the level where I could play pieces of music quite well but was still having to consciously direct my fingers. Then, after years of practice and performance, I began to feel, hear and execute simultaneously when playing a piece of music. In other words, there was no thought between the feeling/hearing and the physical mechanics needed to express it. At this level our body responds directly to feeling without the interference of the mind saying, 'in order to turn left I must turn the steering wheel of my car counter clockwise, do so now'. You just feel the turn and it is done for you. This is the kind of control that the Intelligent Warrior aims for in Martial Art training. However, in Martial Art there is no external device (car, guitar etc.) needed to express yourself – your body is your instrument.

THE LAW OF CONSCiOUS REPETiTiON

We have seen from our various examples that conscious repetition (practice) is the key to the process of embodiment and that it is a law that cannot be transcended. It is not possible to pay somebody lots of money to give you their skills immediately – you could not offer the current snooker champion any amount of money for his skills and expect to be on the professional snooker circuit the same day. Even with the best teachers, *you* have to put the time in, paying attention to the task for many hours (remember the meaning of Kung Fu is 'time spent').

Many people try to hurry the process of embodiment, their expectations of themselves being too high, but if they do not humble themselves in front of or understand the Law of Repetition then they will become disillusioned and fail. There are many unused guitars sitting in various closets all over the world as a result. It is common for people to engage in a skill but then get stuck at some point, unable to improve past that level, or to learn many different skills but only to a rather mediocre level. I am sure most of you have recognized this in others and yourselves.

Understanding the process of embodiment can help us combat this situation. By seeking out new information, teachers and inspirations at the appropriate moments, even when we are bored of practising the skill, we can push through and keep moving forwards. Boredom is the main culprit for eroding our commitment, followed closely by judgment about what or how well we are doing something as compared to someone else. Both of these things involve a serious amount of internal dialogue; applying the skills learned in Meditation to the practice of conscious repetition brings us to the only place where we can effect the process of embodiment, the present moment. By bringing the attention into the body we receive more impressions of what we are trying to do, thus allowing the skill to pass quickly and deeply into us. If you do not embody the music deeply enough when practising it, then when you come to recall it under the pressure of performance it will not be there for you; this also applies to practising Martial Art techniques or any other skill. Persistent quality repetition is the key. The more present and open you are to the experience of embodying something, at any skill level, the more you will be able to deepen the process of embodiment. The deeper the understanding of the skill, the more able you as an Intelligent Warrior will be to express your full capabilities on the battlefield, whether it is the stage, the roads or a conflict situation.

THE THREE CHi KUNG EXERCiSES

All of these exercises are done in the stationary position of the Basic Stance. Try not to allow the movement of the arms to affect the vertical skeletal alignment. All breaths should be inhaled and exhaled through the nose using the Natural Breath Cycle. Try to keep the connection with the feet at all times. Once you have got the basic hang of the exercises, aim to do each movement for at least 16 breaths at a time.

Learning techniques through words and photographs alone is a difficult task. For this reason, try not to rush through the exercises but take one at a time and try to get the feel of the move. If you persevere gradually, the underlying principles (Yin/Yang phases, gravitational pulse and body mechanics) will become clear.

Exercise One: Movement of the Chi

This exercise develops the ability for the hands to move left to right and right to left without disturbing the central core. This is the first movement after your stationary meditation exercise, and for this reason it is made up of half movement and half stillness. Your eyes should continually be trained on the focus point, with the peripheral awareness open. Try to hold the movement and the breath equally in your attention, without losing the connection to your feet on the ground. Try not to allow the movements to affect the Natural Breath Cycle. The moments of stillness with the 'in' breath are the Yin phase, whilst the movements with the 'out' breath are the Yang phase.

1 *Stand in the Basic Stance* (see Photograph 12) *and recall your state of awareness from the end of the Meditation section. This includes connection to the breath, focus point and feet. Also make sure that the angle of the head is correct by tucking your chin in slightly.*

12

13

14

2 *Follow the Natural Breath Cycle in and out using slow rhythmic breathing.*

3 *Follow the breath in and then as you breathe out push the hands up into the position illustrated in Photographs 13 and 14. Keep your hands in that position whilst you breathe in, and then on the 'out' breath move the hands to the right side, keeping the palms over each other (see Photograph 15).*

4 *Remain in that position whilst you breathe in, and then on the 'out' breath push the hands back up into the upright position. Remain there for the 'in' breath, and then on the 'out' breath move the hands to the left side (see Photograph 16). Remain there for the 'in' breath and on the 'out' breath move back up into the upright position.*

5 *Continue this cycle moving left to right for 16 breaths.*

The Intelligent Warrior

15   16

To start with you may need to look at your hands to get positions correct but as soon as you can shift your eyes to the focus point, this will speed up the process of embodiment. Utilizing your skill of Defining the Body, try to open to the sensation of the palms facing each other; the distance between them should not vary. The Chinese called this 'carrying the golden ball' and, in order to increase the attention to the area, suggested you imagine you are holding something very precious between your palms. Initially you may feel the body heat between the palms; after prolonged practice you will feel like two magnets are repelling each other between the palms. Try to control your thumbs as in the photographs – the dynamic tension created by the bend helps to open a major energy pathway known as the Lung Meridian. Once your focus point has been established you should feel no fluctuation in your vertical alignment from left to right as the hands move. Have a sense that your hands are mirroring each other *(see Photograph 14)*.

Exercise Two: Harmonization of the Chi

This exercise is slightly more difficult than the previous one and may take some practice. It is a cyclical move in that there is no rest period. You may wish to practise the double Yuen Sao rotation by itself to start with. It is important that you allow the arms to swing freely at the shoulders as much as possible.

1   *With the hands in the upright position from the last exercise, curl the fingers back towards you while touching your thumb to the tip of your middle finger (see Photographs 17 and 18). Continue to rotate the fingers and wrist (see Photographs 19 and 20) until you return to the upright position (see Photograph 21). The 'in' breath should last the entire duration of the rotation. If you wish to practice this part separately then breathe out when you return to the upright position. This is the double Yuen Sao; after you have got the hang of it, try the rest of the exercise.*

2   *After the rotation, as you are coming back into the upright position, pull the arms back down towards their normal resting position from the Basic Stance. However, keep the hands open and flat, and as you approach the Tan T'ien (see Photograph 22) allow the arms to swing outwards to the side, keeping the wrists in line with the side of the body (see Photograph 23). All of this, including the rotation, should be done on the 'in' breath.*

3   *As you breathe out swing the arms back through exactly the same trajectory as on the 'in' breath, allowing the palms to point upwards slightly into what is known as the double Tan Sao position (see Photograph 24).*

4   *On the 'in' breath start the cycle once again. This exercise is cyclical and can be repeated at will (I would suggest 16 cycles to start with), the hands and arms continually moving with the 'in' and 'out' breaths.*

17

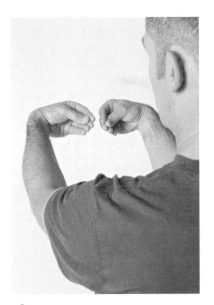

18

19

20

21

22

The Yin phase of this move starts with the double Yuen Sao followed by the hands drawing back in, and is executed while breathing in; the Yang phase starts as the hands move forwards back up into double Tan Sao on the 'out' breath. Again, make sure that the movement of the arms does not pull your spine out of its vertical alignment. Special attention needs to be given to the angle of the head when the arms swing through in the Yang phase as there is a tendency to stick the chin out, thereby putting the cervical vertebra out of alignment. This is a dangerous habit because there will be no 'give' left in the cervical region.

23   24

One of the difficulties in this exercise is to maintain exact hand position whilst having freedom in the shoulder joints. This takes a particular kind of control from the mind (which is very useful for the execution of technique) where an exact message needs to be sent to the hands through the shoulder and arms without making them tense. As you get more adept at this exercise you will begin to feel a gravitational pulse going into the ground as you swing the arms forwards and back. This pulse will feel like you are pushing up from the ground and the pressure will increase momentarily in your feet. To help give you a sense of this try the following exercise.

Tiger Claw Exercise

1   Stand in the Basic Stance but allow the arms to hang by your
    sides.

2   Start swinging the arms simultaneously forwards and back. As
    you do this you should feel the gravitational pulse going into the
    ground.

3   Try to give the legs a little bit of a push upwards as the arms
    swing through. This is almost the same feeling as when on a
    swing, swinging your legs through to propel yourself forwards.

4   Try to power the swing of the arms only by the push of the legs
    and not with the muscles.

This feeling of propelling the arms by the push of the legs is what
you are aiming to achieve in the second exercise. As is mentioned
earlier this exercise combats our tendency to apply force from the
head *(see the Law of Leverage, page 137).*

Exercise Three: Compression of the Chi

This exercise increases force of both the Yin and Yang phases, teaching the body to balance increased force with a complimentary increase in relaxation to ensure correct replenishment of Chi.

1   *In the Basic Stance place the left hand on top of the right and bring them to the level of the solar plexus close to the body (see Photograph 25). As you breathe out press the hands down slowly as if you are pushing down on top of something; you should feel the stomach and diaphragm muscles tense slightly.*

2   *Keep pressing downwards until you reach the level of the Tan T'ien (see Photograph 26) and then snap the hands apart as if what you were imagining to be pushing down on suddenly collapsed. Breathe in at exactly the moment of the snap (see Photograph 27).*

25

26

27   28

3 Allow the hands to push downwards and then circle round (see Photograph 28). The 'in' breath should be quite powerful throughout this movement.
4 As the hands circle round, they come to rest with the left on top of the right at our starting point. Here the cycle begins again.
5 Continue for eight cycles.

The Yang phase occurs as you breathe out and push downwards (the compression phase), the Yin as you snap the movement round and breathe in. As you get better at this move bend the legs slightly as you push downwards and then, as you breathe in, straighten them, returning to your starting position. Be careful not to let any tension creep up into the head and neck area. Because we are trying to increase the muscular force in the diaphragm and core abdominal muscles, there is a tendency for other muscles not used during breathing to tense as well. Try to relax the arms as much as possible in the Yin phase and then increase the tension in the arms during the Yang phase.

Joining the Chi Kung Exercises

After you have become proficient in each of these three exercises separately, join them together so they become one continuous exercise.

29

1   Start from the Basic Stance with the first exercise, pushing up into the upright position.
2   Proceed with the first exercise.
3   After finishing the cycles of the first exercise, go directly into the second without stopping by applying the double Yuen Sao once you are back in the upright position.
4   Proceed with the second exercise.
5   After completing the cycles apply the double Yuen Sao but as you finish the rotation of the wrists flip the left hand on top of the right (see Photograph 29) and bring them into the starting position of the third exercise (see photograph 25). Do this all on the 'in' breath.

30

31

6 Proceed with the third exercise.

7 After completing the cycles, on the snap of the 'in' breath where their hands circle round, instead of circling allow the hands to come up to the 'in' position of the second exercise (see Photograph 30) Push the hands forwards to begin the second exercise again.

8 Complete about half as many cycles of the second exercise as you did before. Apply the double Yuen Sao as if you were starting a new cycle but as you finish the rotation hold the hands in the upright position (see Photograph 31). Begin the first exercise from there.

9 Again, complete about half the number of cycles. Then, as the hands come to the upright position for the last of your cycles, apply the double Yuen Sao and withdraw the hands back into the Basic Stance, fists by the side.

You are practising this now as a cycle, going through the first and second exercises to the third and then returning, halving the number of cycles, through the second and first exercises back to your starting position at the centre. Practising as a cycle allows you to change (transition) from one exercise (manifestation) to the other. This not only teaches the body how to move fluidly from one exercise to another, but also allows you to sense the different character and rhythm of each exercise.

PART THREE

MARTIAL SCIENCE

introduction

Martial Science is the study of the principles that govern a physical confrontation. Similar to the studies of Meditation and Chi Kung, these principles are based on the laws of nature and cannot be transcended. However, whereas Meditation and Chi Kung deal with developing our relationship with our inner and outer worlds, Martial Science deals with our relationship with an opponent. In order to understand this relationship we will study some of the basic laws, strategies and self-defence techniques that govern it. From a wider perspective, the skill and experience gained by understanding Martial Science can be applied to many other situations in your life. In essence, it teaches you to meditate whilst in relation to others so that you can receive clearly what their body, mind and spirit are simultaneously communicating instead of clouding this perception with your own inner reactions (such as thinking about what they are thinking of you). Because you are making powerful movements in Martial Science this can also greatly enhance your general confidence in life and, through the character of the techniques, teach many useful attitudes that resonate with your mind and emotions; for instance, learning how to step out of the way of an oncoming force!

THE LAW OF GRAVITY

We have already spoken at some length about the Law of Gravity. It is a force holding us to the earth and we have to stand upright in the face of it; moreover, this uprightness (verticality) is not permanent and, in times of imbalance (stress, anxiety, fear, overexcitement etc.), humans have a tendency to 'lose' their balance. From the perspective of Martial Science, **the Law of Gravity is important because our opponent is under the same law** and so if our understanding of it is superior to our opponent's, in body, mind *and* spirit, then we will have a distinct advantage. The knowledge that our opponent's verticality is fragile, that they must use a triangular base *(see Align the Body, page 26)* and bipedal motion, and that they must use compensatory movements if they react (for instance, moving their leg when they lean too far forwards), influences how we apply techniques.

This brings us to an important principle that is echoed in Martial Art and esoteric traditions throughout the ages: *in order to know another, one must first know oneself.* This is not a vague mystical statement to be pondered on but rather an extremely practical, scientific principle that, if embodied, can significantly influence the way you orient yourself to your opponent, and ultimately to the world at large. If you can sense the effect that gravity has on you then you will, through your ability to meditate, be able to sense its effect on others (such as, when their foot is about to hit the ground).

Learning how to stand up to somebody or a challenging situation is crucial for attaining your life goals. Conversely, 'crumbling' in front of a problem teaches you how your body instinctively 'goes to ground' when it is overwhelmed or sick.

The Law of Gravity also largely governs the next two laws that we

32

will study: the Law of Momentum and the Law of Leverage

The Law of Momentum states that when an object is put in motion it stays in motion until its energy is spent and will travel in a straight line until another force changes its direction or stops its motion. This is significant in terms of self-defence. When a body moves towards you it must, as we have seen in the Art of Walking, use a triangular base in conjunction with bipedal motion. Think about how you walk. One foot goes in front of the other creating one triangle, and then the rear foot swings through and goes out in front to create another triangle. Whether running, jumping or walking this mechanism must be adhered to; it is a law. Thus, when we set our body in motion and our leg swings through to the front, our body begins to deviate from a straight line as gravity begins to pull the foot down towards the ground. At a point about 5–10 inches away from the ground, the pull is so great that the foot cannot change its direction or stop its downwards motion but must be put down on the ground *(see Photograph 32)*. The sensitivity to this point greatly enhances the timing of techniques – for instance, striking as your opponent's foot hits the ground increases the strike's power because the target is 'falling' onto your striking hand, or if we move our opponent's foot via a 'sweep' or leg trip at the moment where gravity pulls the foot to the ground, the opponent's triangular base will be disturbed, and verticality destabilized.

An assailant must move towards you in order to attack you. The forwards momentum of their body in conjunction with the fact that their foot, as they step in, is pulled to the ground by gravity is termed a Line of Force. The Line of Force dictates that when an opponent attacks from a particular direction they cannot change direction or stop easily. The Sidestep is a technique that takes advantage of this.

THE SIDESTEP

The Sidestep is a primary piece of footwork that changes your
relation to your opponent by adding another plane of movement.
Because the usual reaction is to move backwards away from a
force coming towards you, the Sidestep must be practised.
However, once you have learned how to do it you will be able to
turn 90 degrees sideways, away from the Line of Force. This opens
up completely new possibilities for self-defence and is a quite
closely guarded secret of streetfighters. Let us now look at how
the Sidestep might be done.

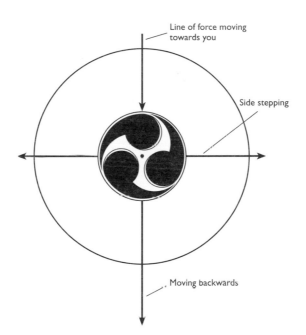

Line of force moving
towards you

Side stepping

Moving backwards

FIGURE 9

33   34

1 Stand in the Basic Stance.
2 Pick up the left foot and turn the heel outwards (see
   Photograph 33). *Step to the Left Neutral (see Photograph 34).*
   Note that your left foot should be positioned at a 45-degree
   angle and the right foot at a slightly sharper 35 degrees (see
   Photograph 35). *Your weight should be evenly distributed*
   between each leg.
3 *Shift your weight slightly to the left leg and pick the right foot*
   up, turning the heel outwards. Shift your weight to the right,
   allowing the right foot to touch the ground toe first. Allow the
   left foot to turn so that your feet end up in the opposite of the
   Left Neutral: the Right Neutral (see Photograph 36).
4 *Continue stepping from Left Neutral to Right Neutral, and then*
   when you feel ready find your focus point and step whilst
   looking at it.

35   36

The Sidestep can buy you valuable time – it may be all you need to slip out of the opponent's way and run away. It brings another dimension into the equation: instead of fighting on one plane (moving forwards and back), we fight on two (left to right and forwards and back). The Sidestep is usually used in conjunction with some form of hand position that either strikes your opponent, locks up their arm or guides them by you. On a psychological level, practising sidestepping gives you practical experience of moving out of the way of force – perhaps an angry customer or partner – and allows the Intelligent Warrior to take the middle path instead of reacting in either a Yang (getting angry back) or Yin (being intimidated or a 'pushover') manner. It opens up the path of nonattachment, which in turn leads to a more intelligent method of resolving conflict.

I have yet to experience an inner or outer conflict situation that could not be resolved by 'rapier wit', 'penetrating insight' or emotional intelligence.

The Line of Force can also be used against your opponent. Due to the Law of Momentum, a body that is in motion cannot stop instantaneously. Therefore, when an attacker is bearing down upon you, the momentum of their weight is moving towards you at a certain speed. If you strike them as they are coming towards you then you will greatly increase the power of your strike – for example, if a car travelling at 30 miles per hour collides head-on with another car travelling at the same speed then the force of the impact is equal to 60 miles per hour. This simple fact is most effective when applying strikes, especially if the striker is of a larger physical stature then you are, as any good boxer will be able to tell you. The Twist Punch *(see page 196)* is a technique that utilizes the Sidestep with a strike back.

THE LAW OF LEVERAGE

The Law of Leverage deals with using the whole body to apply force (Yang) to, or receive force (Yin) from, an opponent. A lever allows one to apply a greater force to move an object than if a force were applied directly. For example, when we pick something up from the ground we are working with the Law of Leverage. If we bend over from the hips and try to pick something up by pulling upwards, we are likely to strain the back because it is not the most efficient way of using the Law of Leverage. However, if we bend at the knees and bring the whole body down we can then use the leverage of the legs to raise the object. This shows that there is a right way and a wrong way to use the body for a particular task, and we can apply this to Martial Science. The most important place where leverage is used by the body is in striking and blocking. The average untrained person will lean in with the upper body and throw a punch with the elbow out *(see the assailant on the left-hand side Photograph 37)*. This is inefficient in several ways:

37

38   39

1   *It means that you have to lift your whole body weight upwards*
    (a) and so it would favour someone with a large body mass, over
    someone with a smaller build who is not going to gain much by
    'throwing his/her weight around'.

2   *By lifting the body weight, you commit more heavily to a line a*
    force, which not only makes your body mechanics easier to
    predict but also destabilizes your centre by lifting up your weight
    and throwing it forwards (b).

3   *If the elbow is pointing out (c) then the energy will not be*
    transferred to the ground (Yin) or, from the opposite perspective,
    you will not be able to lever up from the ground (Yang).

Photograph 38 demonstrates the correct way to use the Law of
Leverage. The power starts from the rear foot on the ground (a); as the
muscles in the rear leg lever upwards, twisting the waist forwards, this
circle increases the energy (b). The elbow is pointing down towards the
rear leg (c) thus allowing it to channel the energy upwards to the hand

(d). Bruce Lee said, 'the rear foot is the piston of the fighting machine', and by this he meant that the power to strike comes from the rear foot and leg. This is much the same as bending your legs down to pick something up. We also see in this example the use of a twisting motion with the waist, which creates a circle that then releases into a straight line via the elbow and hand into the target. This application of circles releasing into a straight line in order to generate force was, and still is, essential to understanding how Kung Fu techniques work. It is a principle that is used in many sports: the swings of a golf club, tennis racket or cricket bat all utilize a circular motion that releases the object (the ball) into a straight line. In fact, David even used it against Goliath.

The same channelling of force used in our example of striking can also be used in the reverse for blocking as in Photograph 39. A force meeting with our blocking hand (a) is transported through the alignment of the elbow (b) down through the rear leg and foot to the ground (c). This is achieved because the force travels through bones that are correctly aligned and so never pushes directly against muscles and/or ligaments. If your bones come out of alignment then muscular exertion will be needed to control the force travelling through the body, which wastes precious energy. In Align the Body we learned how to channel the force of gravity through the bones to the ground, and we can now apply this sensation to both striking and blocking. Moreover, in the second Chi Kung exercise *(see page 154)* we learned to apply force from the centre (Tan T'ien) and not the head. Both striking and blocking depend on the energy channel developed by this exercise and on a stable centre – if the centre is lost even temporarily then the energy of the strike will not reach its full potential.

Embodying the Law of Leverage is one of the most efficient ways of levelling out the differences in body weight, height and mass. Master

Derek Jones evolved the BMS Martial Art system out of the original style of Wing Chun Kung Fu. Nim Wing Chun, the originator of this system, was a 4 foot 10 inch Buddhist nun who, in order to fight off a local gangster's amorous advances (she had actually made a bet with the gangster that if she beat him in hand-to-hand combat he would leave her alone), adapted the system from more traditional Kung Fu styles to suit her diminutive stature. Unfortunately, as with many Kung Fu styles, the present-day Wing Chun has been distorted over its long journey from its roots, and many dubious and modified interpretations have led to a clouding of its original perfect body mechanics. The essence of Nim Wing Chun's original system lay in the alignment of the skeleton, which she embodied after meditating for considerable periods of time on the structure of trees, flowers and the praying mantis insect. (Bruce Lee pays tribute to Nim Wing Chung's influence by including a gambling scene between two praying mantises in the film *Enter The Dragon* where Bruce's superior knowledge earns him a good sum.) The influence of the praying mantis is also quite obvious when observing Nim Wing Chung's greatest gift to Martial Art, the practice of Chi Sao *(see Strategy of Pressure, page 207)*.

When a strike or a block is employed using the Law of Leverage, the body is used as one unit in the same way as when using the correct technique for picking something up. The whole body works together to lever up from the ground and its power is then channelled, in this case through the striking or blocking hand. The emphasis of learning the principles that lie behind techniques, rather than the acquisition of lots of techniques, is essential to correct training in Martial Art, and the body moving as one unit has been a favourite theme in the evolution of Kung Fu. The following is a quote (*circa* 1500 BC) from the Taoist monk Chang San Feng:

The body must move as one single unit

At one with the Breath, Chi and Spirit

The rooting of the feet, the strength
Of the legs,
And the power of the waist all manifest
In the hands
The whole body is connected moving as one
Our movement is guided by our intention

This quote beautifully describes the body moving as one unit, including our breath, Chi and spirit. The feet are rooted to the ground to provide a stable base from which to push upwards, and the large muscles in the legs provide the main thrust, spinning the waist or hip into the strike, through the elbow position and finally manifesting in the hands. Thus, the whole body works together to provide power, not just the arm and the shoulder muscles. Our movement is guided by our intention and comes from the inside. Remember: **before there is any physical movement, there must be an inner impulse or intention to move**. If you are studying Martial Art or, for that matter, any physical discipline, try to ask yourself exactly how your body is working in terms of leverage. When people use leverage in movements it looks effortless and right – the body understands it. Great tennis players, soccer players, batsmen and dancers all have this effortless motion.

If we embody this principle, many movements that we make when applying force to something will be transformed, for example, opening doors, sawing a piece of wood, scrubbing a countertop or pushing a car. By practising Martial Art techniques that employ the correct principles of leverage, such as the second Chi Kung exercise and the Twist Punch, the body learns to support the hands through its centre of gravity. As this way of moving takes root in the body of attention, it begins to impose itself on our everyday movements, slowly transforming them. However, if you do not support your hands in the correct (natural) way, then eventually injury will occur. When we use unnatural body mechanics the force is not conducted up from or down to the ground cleanly through the centre. As mentioned in the aligning the body section, if our spine is misaligned in any way then part of the force will get 'stuck' at the point of misalignment thereby causing injury to the vertebra. Back and neck injuries are the most common result of leverage misuse; other injuries that can occur from bad leverage are pulled muscles, strained or ripped ligaments, skeletal dislocations, hernias, fallen arches and arthritis.

Studying the Law of Leverage teaches the Intelligent Warrior not to use excessive force when trying to achieve a goal, whether that be defeating an opponent or winning over work colleagues with an idea. If you have to force something or someone then you are approaching it in the wrong way and you need to get 'more leverage' on the situation.

Now we have looked at some of the basic laws that govern self-defence we can begin to study the techniques and the strategies we use to employ them.

strategy of distance

The maintenance of proper fighting distance has a decisive effect on the outcome of the fight — acquire the habit! **Bruce Lee (1975)**

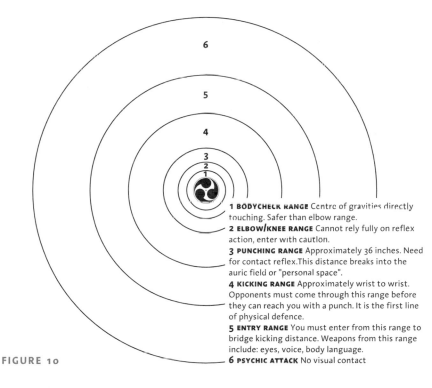

1 BODYCHECK RANGE Centre of gravities directly touching. Safer than elbow range.

2 ELBOW/KNEE RANGE Cannot rely fully on reflex action, enter with caution.

3 PUNCHING RANGE Approximately 36 inches. Need for contact reflex. This distance breaks into the auric field or "personal space".

4 KICKING RANGE Approximately wrist to wrist. Opponents must come through this range before they can reach you with a punch. It is the first line of physical defence.

5 ENTRY RANGE You must enter from this range to bridge kicking distance. Weapons from this range include: eyes, voice, body language.

6 PSYCHIC ATTACK No visual contact

FIGURE 10

A strategy is a set of ideas that you can apply to a seemingly chaotic situation to bring order to it. By so doing we begin to limit some of the variables that could go wrong. The Strategy of Distance develops a practical sense of the three-dimensional space around us in the application of self-defence techniques. This strategy can also be applied to other, less violent, situations in our lives, such as somebody entering or violating our personal space, or sexual harassment in the workplace. Another application is: becoming aware of the distances between you and other people. For instance, on a crowded train platform, in order to avoid an accident or being pickpocketed. By gaining a sense of distance, we can take advantage of an opponent who has less sensitivity to it and so gain the advantage in a conflict situation. Its application relies upon the skills developed in Meditation, Chi Kung and Martial Science, and our perception of two main factors: time and distance.

The underlying principle of the Strategy of Distance is that for an assailant to attack you, he must move towards you, and as he moves towards you, he must cross over finite distances to physically reach you. As the distance decreases between you and your opponent so too does the time available to you for counterattack. These distances can be seen as concentric circles (as you can be attacked from any direction) emanating out from your centre *(see Figure 10)*. For each distance there are corresponding techniques, for example, kicking techniques at kicking distance, punching techniques at punching distance, and so on. If the wrong technique is used at a particular distance, for example, trying to punch someone at kicking distance, then a strategic error has been committed. If your opponent commits a strategic error, you should be able to bring the conflict to a swift and favourable resolution by employing the Strategy of Distance correctly. It is possible, through practice, to develop one's sense of distance to a very high level, and this

 The Intelligent Warrior

development is essential because our ability to judge time and distance is severely disrupted in conflict situations. However, before embarking upon a study of the various significant distances and their accompanying techniques, we need to understand where one best needs to be 'placed' within oneself in order to gain an exact sense of distance.

Our ability to judge time and distance precisely is directly proportionate to the stability of our centre. A stable centre, as developed through Meditation and Chi Kung, allows us to stabilize ourselves in the three-dimensional space. As your centre stabilizes through your presence, your sensitivity will increase, via your senses, to any object moving within the three-dimensional space in relation to the concentric circles outlined earlier. The increased sense of ourselves in relation to the three-dimensional space allows us to 'draw a line in the sand', stop moving around and make a stand in a particular place; for example, we stop backing away from an aggressor. This results in two immediate effects: it creates a subtle force that goes back towards the aggressor and it allows us to judge distance with precision. The force that is projected back towards the aggressor is a balance between Yin and Yang; it is neither aggressive nor passive. If you are intimidated, your awareness and sense of self contracts, and you will start to withdraw inside yourself by looking or backing away, or engaging in internal conversation; this is an instinctual form of defence and, because it involves contraction, is classified as a Yin reaction. A Yang reaction, on the other hand, would be to meet force with force, in other words, if you sense that you are being aggressed you will respond with aggression back. Both of these reactions are dangerous: a Yin reaction means that we will not be aware of the aggressor's attack, which tends to make the aggressor feel powerful and so they will continue their attack (this is often the cause of long-term abuse within the family unit); a Yang reaction, on the other hand, will tend to start a physical confrontation where there does not need to be one – it tends to 'wind' the aggressor up, causing an escalation and thereby increasing the chances of an argument 'blowing up in your face', or of being injured or killed. Most people fall into one or other of these categories, but the Intelligent Warrior learns how to cultivate a balance between these complementary opposites. This allows the Intelligent Warrior to stand still in front of an aggressor, unmoved by their violent intentions, challenging them with their presence (Yang) and yet at the same time opening and receiving all the subtle and not so subtle clues that they are manifesting as to their intentions (Yin). The awareness of the Yin and Yang principle in this situation allows us to judge distance with more precision. Bringing the body to a point of stillness means that there is only one moving variable (the aggressor) instead of two (both you and the aggressor), which makes the judgment of distance from the point of stillness much easier. Our heightened perception of this, plus our sensitivity to their movements, allows us to decisively employ, via the correct techniques, the Strategy of Distance.

When we 'still' our body in front of an aggressor, it is essential that we put it into a form conducive to the execution of our techniques, and this shape is dependent upon their mode of attack. There are two basic ways that someone will attack you:

1 *The aggressor will try to intimidate you with their voice and gestures, closing the space between you with their hands down (see Photograph 40) or at least not in a striking posture. In this case, use the Trigger Position (see page 185).*

2 *The aggressor will come directly at you with their hands or feet*

'winding up' for a strike, grab or kick (see Photograph 41). In this
case, use the On-guard Position (see Photographs 42 and 43).

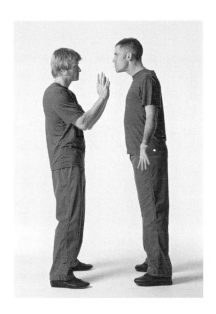 

40   41

In both these positions, the focus point developed in Meditation
now goes between your opponent's eyes, just below the level of the
eyebrow. This protects against looking directly into their eyes,
which would have the tendency to distract us by eliciting emotions
of a personal nature (making you feel that the aggressor does not
like you and wants to hurt you). Having found this focus point
(specific sight or Yang) you then open your peripheral awareness
(nonspecific sight or Yin) to take in their whole body, making sure
you include their five points of coordination. This allows you to
perceive their body as a whole unit. This awareness will then alert
you to subtle clues in the body mechanics they are about to employ
for their attack and allows you to intercept their strike at an early
stage. For example, if they begin to clench their right hand, contort
their face and widen their eyes whilst beginning to step across

kicking distance, we can sense their intention to employ a right-hand punch, and can prepare a more appropriate technique for this range (the Front Kick) to cut their strike off at kicking distance, rather than waiting for their punch to come into punching distance and blocking it. The use of time and distance as a weapon was

42

43

extremely important for Bruce Lee, so much so that he named his style Jeet Kune Do, which translated means 'the way of the intercepting fist'. By this, he meant your fist intercepts your opponent's attack, and ends it at the earliest opportunity.

We will now study in more detail the actual distances and corresponding self-defence techniques utilized within the Strategy of Distance.

The Intelligent Warrior

On-guard Position

The On-guard Position is the basic 'ready' position. If your opponent approaches you in a fighting stance (hands raised or in the process of being raised) then you take the On-guard Position.

1   Stand in the Left Neutral
2   Raise your hands (see Photographs 34 and 35). Extend the left hand forwards (Yang) with a 135-degree bend at the elbow, and position the right hand just by the left elbow (Yin).
3   The left hand should be placed between your face and the focus point, while remaining focused on the focus point.
4   Also practise the mirror image of this in the Right Neutral, with the right hand up and your left hand placed between your face and your opponent's face.

The Trigger Position

Many acts of aggression start with a less obvious form of intimidation. An aggressor may approach you with intimidating body language, verbal abuse, compliments or guile. In such cases, it is best to take a stance that provides you with protection but is not obviously a Martial Art pose. If you assume an obvious Martial Art stance too early then you could provoke a confrontation or be seen as the aggressor (causing possible legal problems in the future), plus you do not want to lose the element of surprise by letting the aggressor see that you know how to defend yourself. At the same time, you need to have a position that can provide you with protection in an instant. In a sense, this position is a form of camouflage as it allows you to hide behind common body language until your opponent triggers your self-defence technique. The Trigger Position is the best position for this:

44

1 Stand with your feet parallel and slightly apart, with your weight evenly distributed, and in as natural position as possible.

2 Bring your hands up in front of your heart area and gently touch the hands together (see Photograph 44), again as naturally as possible.

3 Find the focus point between your opponent's eyes, sink your weight down slightly and connect to your breathing.

4 Practise the Twist Punch (see page 196) and Front Kick (see page 192) starting from this position as opposed to from an On-guard Position.

The Trigger Position can be used in almost every situation that you find yourself in (such as in bars, on trains, at bus stops or along pavements). It can be used at any time when you are accosted but are unsure whether the person in front of you is intent on using physical violence. **Note: The main reason why people are caught unaware by a strike when confronted with a conflict situation is that they do not know how to prepare for the possibility of physical attack, have no strategy and do not know where to look or put their hands, let alone defend themselves**. Through the processes of Meditation, Chi Kung and Martial Science, you will have experienced what it means to have inner form, and this will allow you now to have outer form in a conflict situation. I stress again that the inner form *must* come before the outer – you *must* understand what is happening within before any external technique can work efficiently. The inner form gained by practising the Trigger Position allows the Intelligent Warrior to learn how to 'shape shift' (an American Indian term) efficiently. This means that after you have become used to holding inner form in the face of aggression you can *consciously* shape your outer form to take any appropriate shape (such as a gesture, facial expression or self-defence technique) to disarm the situation.

Entry Distance

Entry Distance, so called because the opponent enters from here into the range of your self-defence techniques, is the longest distance in the Strategy of Distance and therefore gives you the most time to react. It is the distance where your opponent is within visual and aural range but cannot physically reach you, and it begins just outside the Kicking Distance. However, they can still attack you from this range using verbal and emotional abuse. Stimuli such as these impact upon the senses and can cause acute reactions in the body such as agitation, denial and even paralysis. Many attackers will probe you from this distance to see whether you are a good candidate for their aggression. It is imperative that you immediately activate your presence if you find yourself in this scenario – too many people end up being hurt because they refuse to accept early enough that they are in a confrontational situation. **Remember: awareness is your first line of defence, presence is the second.** Utilize your peripheral awareness to watch, listen and sense your assailant but keep any direct communication with them short and to the point. Since this is the longest distance, you have the most time to make decisions, and it is here where you decide to either remove yourself from the situation (Yin) with awareness, or to engage the aggressor with your presence (Yang) in the form of meeting their gaze, 'piercing' them with your rapier wit/insight or asking 'penetrating' questions.

Gaining experience of Entry Distance teaches the Intelligent Warrior to be aware of an approaching problem at the earliest opportunity so as to be able to apply an intelligent strategy to it.

 The Intelligent Warrior

Kicking Distance

If you decide to stay in this particular scenario and your assailant moves towards you, they will move from the Entry Distance to the next significant self-defence range: the Kicking Distance. This is the first distance from where you can physically reach the opponent with your longest weapon: the Front Kick. The Front Kick is arguably your most useful weapon as it counteracts the most common form of attack: a rear hand strike from the right-hand side. As a general rule, if your assailant moves through this distance with their hands down and without any overt signs of physical aggression, assume the Trigger Position. However, if their hands are up in a striking or grabbing pose then apply the Front Kick directly to the groin. In either scenario, you must find the focus point *(see page XXX)* between the eyes and activate your peripheral awareness. Utilizing the focus point in this technique stops you from looking down at the target (the groin), which is by far the most common 'telegraph' (the Martial Art terminology for a small clue elicited by someone just before or during an attack, which gives away their intention). The Front Kick deals with the most common strategic error made by an assailant, which is using a short-range weapon at a long range, such as a punch at kicking range.

The Front Kick

45

46

1   Stand in the left On-guard Position (see Photograph 45).

2   Drop the left hand down and move to the side, dragging your left toe along the ground (see Photograph 46).

3   Lift the left knee directly upwards from the hip, keeping the knee joint loose (see Photograph 47).

4   'Snap' the left foot (pull the toes back as you do this) out simultaneously with the left hand (see Photograph 48).

5   Allow your weight to fall forwards and land in the Front Stance (see Photograph 49).

6   Practise this starting from the right as well as the left On-guard Position until you feel the movement of the leg, including the snap, as one continuous movement, breathing in as you move the leg across and upwards and breathing out as you snap. Try to feel this movement as a curve that releases into the snap, a bit like a pitcher in baseball or a bowler in cricket uses the circular movement of the arm to 'snap' the ball through.

47

48

49

Application of the Front Kick

1 As your opponent moves across Kicking Distance, their hands will begin to rise into striking or grabbing positions. As they do this, begin the Front Kick (see Photographs 50 and 51).

50

51

2 Immediately, without stopping, apply the Front Kick.

3 Land and strike simultaneously (see Photograph 52).

52

The Intelligent Warrior

The snapping movement (called Bil Sao) with the lead hand clears any hand that is in your way of the centre line, opening the possibility for attack by your hands. Because it looks very similar to a hand striking, it also acts as a decoy by engaging your opponent's vision, thus leaving the foot to connect with its target unnoticed. The snapping action of the hand and foot also generates force (via circles releasing into straight lines), utilizing a relatively small amount of movement. Pulling the toes back provides a wider striking area on the foot and prevents the force from impacting on the tip of the toes where it will cause injury.

The Front Kick is one of the most important techniques to master and the one that I have used more than any other in conflict situations. Practising it teaches the Intelligent Warrior to use the appropriate tool for the job – many large jobs look daunting at face value but if you see what is needed and apply the correct tool then the job is soon 'cut down to size'.

Punching Distance

Your assailant has come across the Kicking Distance with their hands down and may be abusive, smiling, asking you questions or even complimenting you. At the edge of the Auric Field (the electrical field that emanates approximately 36 inches from your body) your assailant stops advancing. This is shorter than kicking distance and therefore you have less time to react. You should be in the Trigger Position, keeping your peripheral awareness focused on their hands and, if they are being verbally abusive, grounding the energy through your feet. If they are asking questions or are beguiling in any manner, do not be 'taken in' by their words. If they reach to strike or grab you, apply the following Twist Punch.

The Twist Punch

53

54

55

56

1 Take the left On-guard Position (see Photograph 53).

2 Turn the right hand slowly into a fist as you extend it out towards the focus point whilst slowly moving the left hand to the Jut Sao Position (see Photograph 54).

3 As the right hand extends you will feel it begin to pull the right shoulder round, and when you feel this, lift the right foot and sidestep to a Right Neutral (see Photographs 55 and 56).

4 Practise the opposite Twist Punch by starting in the Right Neutral.

The Twist Punch has its roots in Wing Chung Kung Fu and follows the same principles for punching that were outlined in the Law of Leverage – the thrust comes up from the ground, which utilizes a powerful twisting action from the waist (circle) that is transferred through the elbow and released into a straight punch (straight line). Because you are striking your opponent as they are moving towards you, your strike will be travelling into the Line of Force *(see page XXX)*, which increases its power. If practised correctly it is a highly effective technique that can deal with any kind of punch or grabbing action.

When you are proficient at doing the Twist Punch from the On-guard Position, try going directly from one Twist Punch to another. In order to do this the punching hand turns directly into a Jut Sao and the Jut Sao turns directly into a punch.

57

1 Stand in Trigger Position.

2 As the opponent raises their hand to strike, sidestep away from the striking hand by applying the Twist Punch (see Photograph 57).

58

3 Aim to connect the punch just under the cheekbone (see Photograph 58).

The Fence

One more technique needs to be added to our arsenal: the Fence Position. If we return to Figure 10 *(see page 179)*, you will see that the next distance inwards from the Punching Distance is the Elbow and Knee Range, most commonly entered when an attacker tries to intimidate by putting their face right up in front of yours, and you should avoid this at all costs. At this range you cannot use your peripheral awareness, cannot see their legs or hands and, if you are smaller than the attacker, then they will be bearing down upon you. In order to combat this situation, study the following technique.

59

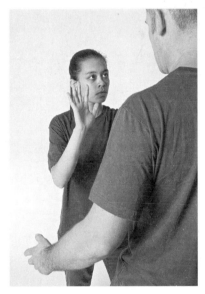

60

1 *Stand in the Trigger Position.*
2 *Step back with the right foot, lifting the left hand and gently placing it in the middle of your assailant's chest, whilst moving the right hand slightly back with an open palm and fingers* (see Photographs 59 and 60).

61

3   *If you sense your attacker striking, leave the left hand on the chest and strike directly into their head by turning the open right hand into a punch as its moves towards their head (see Photograph 61). This should be done utilizing a sharp 'out' breath through the nose as you punch.*

4   Return the right hand back to its original position.

 The Intelligent Warrior

One of the things that a Fence Position does is to alert people around you to a potential conflict. For instance, somebody standing extremely close to you in a crowded bar would not look so unusual, but the moment you step back and put a hand up in front of them other people will start to notice – CCTV cameras will pick up your gesture and so will bar and security personnel. In addition, any witnesses present will see that you are not promoting violence, so if you do happen to cause personal injury then you are much less likely to be bothered from a legal perspective later. The Fence Position puts a physical barrier up between you and your aggressor; often it is enough to make your aggressor 'stall'. By this, I mean that if your aggressor wants to continue to move forwards towards you, they must first remove your hand, thus initiating physical combat. Very often, the person does not have enough 'balls' to do this, so they stall and repeatedly make verbal threats. If this occurs then give them a way out, perhaps by saying, 'look friend there is no problem, just leave it out' or by making a joke, thereby avoiding full physical confrontation.

The Fence Position is essential for teaching the Intelligent Warrior how to protect their immediate personal space and how to 'draw a line in the sand'. There comes a time in any conflict, whether verbal or physical, when we say enough is enough. The Fence Position is an alarm that says you must protect yourself *now*, and is your last real opportunity to apply strategy to the conflict before the conflict becomes physically violent.

Energy Reversal

The previous three techniques – the Front Kick, Twist Punch and Fence Position – are known as Energy Reversal techniques. This means that the flow of energy or force that your opponent has initiated towards you is reversed as *your* energy (from the punch or kick) impacts into them, driving them backwards. This is a significant moment in a conflict situation because up until this point you have had to deal with their energy coming towards you.

For example, you are minding your own business, standing at a bus stop, when your awareness senses somebody approaching in your direction (the energy is moving towards you). You hold them in your peripheral awareness until it is obvious that they are about to accost you in some way, so you turn and assume the Trigger Position, bringing your presence to bear (their energy is focused specifically upon you). The person approaches you asking for some money, you deny them and they get agitated and insulting (the energy level has risen) – you are beginning to experience what is known in the bouncing industry as the 'adrenalin dump'. The natural chemicals of the fight-or-flight response are flying into your system – your heart rate is rising, you are feeling flushed, your legs are shaking and your voice is wavering. As the person moves into Punching Distance, you prepare yourself for the likelihood of a physical attack. Your peripheral awareness picks up that the assailant's hands are beginning to clench into fists, and then they begin to raise one of their hands to strike (the energy is about to manifest itself as a physical attack). You immediately apply the Twist Punch, a move where you both block and attack at the same time, and your fist connects with the assailant's head, knocking them backwards. The energy has now reversed and is moving away from you.

Right from the start, as the impression of an aggressive person 'hits' your three primary senses, the body realizes the possibility of an attack and reacts accordingly. However, through the process of Meditation that fight-or-flight reaction is not enough to disintegrate you. You hold yourself together enough to apply technique and at that moment, the energy moves away from you for the first time; this is the point where you must either run away or continue to attack and neutralize your opponent. However, since the common human reaction is to stop after reversing the energy flow, you need to train yourself to use your fight-or-flight response for fighting or running away.

So now you have a complete picture. Your awareness alerts you to *potential* trouble before it has become a threat aimed directly at you. If the situation does evolve into a threat focused directly on you then your presence allows you to channel the energy released by the fight-or-flight response, which in turn allows you to judge distance more effectively. Awareness of both the distance that your opponent is crossing and the body mechanics they are using to move allows you to apply the appropriate technique to reverse the energy. As the energy (the person) starts to move away from you, you either end the conflict by removing yourself from the immediate vicinity (by running away), or you continue to drive the offending person away by continuing your attack until they submit or take flight themselves. This is all the Strategy of Distance and to make it work takes practice and experience. Do not think that reading is going to change anything immediately because it will not, and that assumption could be a very costly one. However, the premise that the strategy is built on is sound, simple and straightforward, and in order to make the strategy work you must embody it.

Energy Reversal teaches the Intelligent Warrior to take opportunities when they arise, which might be sensing that you are winning a discussion and then pressing your point home, or closing a sale.

Further Techniques

GROUND FiGHTiNG

Some martial artists advocate going to the ground (grappling) as a form of fighting, but I do not recommend it. Ground fighting does have its place, especially if you are contemplating doing any kind of security work in clubs and bars where it is an essential skill, but the scope of this book does not allow us to go into it. It is my assertion that it is better to spend your valuable time working on developing a sense of balance and, in so doing, learning how to stay on your feet. My reasons are as follows:

1 *If you go to the ground and your opponent remains on their feet they can then use the force of gravity against you most obviously by kicking you, dropping things on you or using any blunt weapon against you more effectively. However, in your average street encounter it is quite difficult for somebody to hurt you badly when you are standing up – you might get a bloody nose, a cut or a black eye, but real internal damage is quite rare. Your opponent has to have a very good punch or simply get very lucky in order to really hurt you (most serious head injuries occur as the head hits the ground) when you are standing up, but the moment you go to the ground even a drunken idiot can do you a lot of harm.*

2 *If you go to the ground, it is very difficult for any passers-by to see you. If you scream or cry out passers-by could look over but would not be able to see you if you are behind an obstacle such as a hedge or car. If you choose to run away, you must first bring yourself back up to the upright position, which may not be easy. There could be glass on the ground or cars manoeuvring and so on.*

3 *Being on your feet facing your opponent keeps them at bay as there is a natural force field that they have to breach. If there is*

*more than one opponent there is usually a ringleader who has a
bit more balls than the rest – the others tend to be hangers-on and
not quite as brave. However, if you go to the ground then the
others will suddenly get all kinds of courage and start attacking
you like a pack of dogs. There is a case for the effectiveness of
ground fighting in a one-on-one situation but it is close to useless
when there are multiple opponents.*

RUNNiNG AWAY

There is one other way of relating to your opponent's Line of Force
that needs mentioning, that is running away. I have seen some
ridiculous books and videos that advocate running away as a primary
form of self-defence; this is madness or at best plain ignorance of
the reality of conflict situations. Running away is one of our
instinctual methods for self-defence given to us by nature as part of
the fight-or-flight response, and will take over if you lose your
centre. In itself, running away is not bad. There is no loss of face in
street fights, only survival – it is better to run away than to be
seriously injured or die. However, you must be very careful when
using it as a strategic form of self-defence as the moment you turn
your back on an assailant your awareness for the most part is taken
away – you can perhaps hear them, but you cannot see them.
Therefore, unless you have trained your ears to a high degree, you
will not know where or how far behind you they are, nor will you
know whether they have pulled out a weapon. Also, as mentioned
earlier when looking at the negative effects of going to the ground
if there are multiple opponents, if you stand and face them it keeps
them to some degree at bay, perhaps long enough for a passer-by to
help or for another exit to present itself to you. The moment you
turn away from them, as with going to the ground, the people who

were afraid to attack you directly will come after you like a pack of wolves.

If you do start to run, try to be sure about where you are running to. In a conflict situation both your energy levels and how your body uses that energy are instinctively changed. Your body goes into a mode that immediately gives you the maximum amount of energy – you do not want to deplete this energy by running away, only to be caught 50 yards down the road when you are out of breath. You must learn to measure your energy carefully. If, with your peripheral awareness, you can see, say, a lit street or a group of people that is a reasonable distance away, then by all means try to create a distraction and bolt for it. However, to run away indiscriminately can land you in a worse situation then you were before. Many muggers actually like you to run away so that they can run up behind you and push you forwards to the ground where you will end up face down with no options for self-defence, as opposed to face up, on your back, with at least some options.

strategy of
pressure

The seeing commit a strange error. They believe
that we know the world only through our eyes. For
my part, i discovered that the universe consists
of pressure, that every object and every living
being reveals itself to us at first by a kind of
quiet yet unmistakable pressure to indicate its
intention and its form.   Lusseyran (1999: 28)

When the opponent expands i contract, when he
contracts i expand, and when there is an
opportunity, i do not hit it hits all by itself.
Bruce Lee in *Enter the Dragon* (1973)

The Strategy of Pressure deals with laws of expansion and
contraction and our ability to hold the two in balance. In terms of
Martial Art, it is the doorway to another dimension and could justify
having a book written on it alone. Pressure is the primary way that
the physical world communicates itself to us, and by developing a
sensitivity to it we begin to speak a new 'energetic' language with a
speed of communication that far outstrips our usual language of

conscious thought. Working with this strategy develops pressure-sensitive triggers that gradually take over the initiation and control of technique from the visual pathway that uses intellectual recognition. The starting point for this kind of development is the sense of touch, or kinaesthetics, that was introduced in Outer Meditation *(see page 105)*; we now put that skill to use by 'listening' to our opponent. What is presented here is just a brief glimpse of the subject, but you will be able to get a feel for where this kind of training might take you.

An impression that comes through our sense of touch does not travel through the same neural pathway as a visual one; in fact it travels a path that relates more directly to our cerebellum, which is the part of the mind that controls smooth movement. For this reason, the sense of touch is exceptionally well equipped to trigger and control movement. Our usual way of perceiving attack is through the sense of sight; however, the eyes have a much greater tendency to connect to the intellectual part of the brain. This increases the danger of thinking about a move rather than immediately making it. Using the sense of touch bypasses the whole conscious recognition mechanism where the eyes receive an impression, communicate it to the brain, and then recognize it, for instance, as a punch. The brain responds by trying to choose an appropriate technique to deal with the perceived threat. Bypassing this mechanism is necessary because the energy rises in a conflict situation and seriously disrupts the complicated communication needed for this process of recognition, which in turn makes the application of a Martial Art technique close to impossible. Developing the sense of touch builds what is known as a 'contact reflex', which, as the name suggests, is a reflex that fires on contact with the skin. This is similar to the reflex that pulls your hand away from a flame when it gets too near or makes you blink when something approaches your eye. Correct Martial Art training endeavours to supplant these instinctive reflexes with reflexive 'techniques'.

Reflexive techniques can be broken down into those that expand and those that contract. For example, if I am touching my opponent and they pulls their hand away, the decrease of pressure on my arm instantaneously fires an expanding technique such as a strike. However, if my opponent suddenly pushes in on me, or their strike hits my arm, my reflex fires a retreat or block as I contract away from them. This is what Bruce Lee meant when he said, 'I don't hit, it hits all by itself'. With time, contact reflex becomes a fluid connection that reads your opponent's intention continuously from the moment you touch them, rather than just when they strike or pull away. For this to happen you need to have developed an impeccable sensitivity or balance between expansion and contraction.

62

Traditionally in Kung Fu this contact reflex is trained in the practice of Chi Sao or 'sticking hands' (see Photograph 62). In Chi Sao the practitioners spend a long time working through a series of routines that involve striking and blocking whilst touching somebody else's arms. These routines become increasingly random and varied so that it soon becomes impossible for our normal thought processes to control the movements. Through this touch they learn to feel their opponent's intention, even before this intention has the chance to move the physical body. This develops another kind of sight in the body or perhaps a more appropriate way of saying it would be another sense of hearing. The practitioner literally 'listens' to the person through their arms. After a prolonged period of practice, or conscious repetition, the practitioner can instantaneously glean an incredible amount of information from just touching their opponent's arm, such as the body's size, weight, alignment and muscle density plus more elusive areas such as emotional type, emotional agitation and intention. The development of this works in much the same way as a blind person who quite instinctively develops the other senses to compensate for their 'handicap':

> When I awakened my attention, however, every tree immediately came to me. This must be taken quite literally. Every single tree projected its form, its weight, its movement – even if it was almost motionless – in my direction. I could indicate its trunk, and the place where its first branches started, even when several feet away. By and by something else became clear to me, and this can never be found in books. The world exerts pressure on us from the distance.
>
> Lusseyran, 1999: 28)

The Intelligent Warrior

This passage points to the possible evolution of communication through the energetic language of pressure, an awakening to higher levels of sensitivity that is one of the primary functions of art in general. When somebody expands towards you, the air molecules between you compress, and when they contract, a vacuum is created; the body is quite capable of becoming sensitive to this movement of air. At this level, you can 'feel' what your opponent is doing, moreover this heightened sense of touch begins to work more and more in conjunction with peripheral vision and hearing, melding into an overall state of awareness *(see The Seamless Web of Awareness, page 124)*.

The effect on our daily lives from this kind of training can be quite profound. There are moments when we need to 'grab the bull by the horns' or take an opportunity that presents itself and, conversely, there are times when we need to retreat or at least hold back in order to gather more information so as not to 'go off half cocked'. The decision whether you, as poker players say, 'hold them' or 'fold them' can have a substantial impact on your life. We all engage in internal conversation about opportunities we should have taken or things we feel we should not have done. The Strategy of Pressure lies at the heart of intelligence, with the ability to sense the balance between opposites, such as expansion and contraction, the breath in and the breath out, the yes and the no, the left and the right, the up and the down, the Yin and the Yang, and then to allow the present moment to dictate your decision on which direction to be intended.

THE ART OF WAR

> So a military force has no constant formation,
> water has no constant shape: the ability to gain
> victory by changing and adapting according to the
> opponent is called genius.   **Tzu (1988: 113)**

China has a very long history of war and social upheaval. The leaders of various dynasties and clans relied heavily on advisers in both making battle plans and controlling their subjects. What is interesting about this is that, as well as soldiers, philosophers and spiritual masters were also employed for this job. Confucius and Lao Tzu both held significant government posts; Bodidharma came to China because he had been summoned to advise the current emperor. This led to a much deeper understanding of the nature of warfare and human engineering, and this understanding bears much resemblance to our concept of holistic self-defence. There is a tremendous amount of literature written about the subject most notably Sun Tzu's, *The Art of War*. This book, written over 2000 years ago, is still a bestseller and used by businesspeople, corporations and sports teams all over the world, which is a testament to the depth of understanding of its author.

A simple analogy of a battlefield can serve to illustrate the connection between full-scale battle strategy and our concept of holistic self-defence: the first thing a commander of an army does on becoming aware of an impending battle is to gather facts –scouts are sent out to study the weather, terrain, available weapons, numbers of troops, and the ability for mobility of his and the enemy's army. These facts are brought to him from the outside world in its present state at that time and represent awareness.

Next they must become aware of their own army (body), for instance, how many and what type of troops are available to them, and lines of communication (nerves) must be set up. They must also ensure that their supply lines are intact so that the army will not run out of energy (Chi). In addition, they themselves must not express signs of fear when they learn about the enemy, otherwise troops will lose moral. This stage represents **presence**. After gathering facts and taking 'stock' of the situation, they must then form a **strategy** for dealing with the enemy and in order to implement the strategy a variety of troops must be deployed. These troops have weapons, some long-range (kicks), some medium-range (punches) and some short-range (knees), and depending on the skill of the troops and how well they are deployed they can take advantage of strategic errors made by their opponents (**Martial Science**). However, all good commanders know that when the battle begins the army must be fluid and able to adapt. It must know when to press forwards (Yang), when to retreat (Yin) and when to stay still (balance), for this ability allows them to feel in the present moment the ebb and flow of their opponents (**Martial Art**). In this analogy, we see the understanding of the laws governing a combat situation, the strategies involved and the actual techniques used to manifest the strategy.

On a smaller scale, you are the commander and you will be employing the strategies of distance and pressure and using some self-defence techniques to deploy your strategy. The quality of your commander, scouts and troops is dependent upon the depth of understanding or 'embodiment' of the Meditation and Chi Kung sections for it is here that you are strengthened as an individual (indivisible duality). Thomas Cleary describes *The Art of War* as *'a study of the anatomy of organisations in conflict'*, saying it *'applies to competition and conflict in general, on every level from the interpersonal to the international'*. We are taking that one step further with the concept of holistic self-defence in which our body, mind and spirit comprise an organisation. In fact, Sun Tzu's advice to medical wisdom was:

> ... to foil the enemy's plots is like keeping healthy so as to be resistant to disease; to ruin their alliances is like avoiding contagion; to attack their armed forces is like taking medicine; to besiege their cities is like performing surgery.
>
> **Tzu (600 BC)**

Whether it is countries at war, groups of people arguing, person to person conflict or conflict between the various personalities within our own bodies, the science of martial situations is the same.

PART FOUR

MARTIAL ART

I hope martial artists are more interested in the roots of martial arts and not the different decorative branches, flowers or leaves. It is futile to argue as to which single leaf, which designs of branches or which attractive flower you like; when you understand the root, you understand all it is blossoming.   **Bruce Lee (1975)**

introduction

The final area of study is Martial Art, which is the culmination of all that has been learned, understood and embodied in the previous sections of this book and, as with any art, is about self-expression. In the art of music the musician 'pays attention' for years, mastering his instrument and embodying the principles of music, but if the process is to be completed then at some point he must eventually step on stage in front of an audience and express himself. A direct product of the quality of a musician's preparation is how free the musician is to express himself authentically and honestly to 'strike a chord' with each member of the audience. Martial artists are involved in exactly the same process, with the only difference being that the theatre in which they perform or operate is not confined to a raised platform but encompasses all life's scenarios, songs and scene changes. In much the same way as musicians try to 'win an audience over' or 'knock them dead', martial artists challenge themselves and their immediate worlds or 'spheres of influence' by communicating and affecting the action/reaction cycle which is, as we have seen, an unavoidable reality of our existence. In this way, intelligent warriors learn to adapt their awareness (Yin) and expression or presence (Yang) to any situation or 'theatre' that their lives present them with. The two basic situations in life that require martial artists' attention are things that happen which are beyond their control and things that they consciously choose to challenge (remember the definition of 'warrior'). Most of us have not been born into a life where we must go out and actually participate in a real war, where that life could be ended in an instant. Nevertheless, we face many battles in our day-to-day life that are very real. By studying the principles in this book it is my wish that you find a way to become more efficient at dealing with your daily battles, whether fighting for what you want out of life, defending yourself against habitual negative thoughts and emotions or actually dealing with another human aggressing you.

Nature offers us many examples of life forms that adapt and express themselves appropriately to their environments in order to survive, such as the ability of the chameleon to change colour, an animal's instinct to hunt or the roots of a tree seeking water. The originators of Kung Fu meditated upon 'scenarios' where life forms adapted themselves to their environments in order to survive. The simple expression of a flower is often referred to in Taoist writings, and is one that we have used before – the flower head (Martial Art) can only exist and adapt to the sunlight with the support of its stem (Chi Kung and Martial Science) and its roots in the earth (Meditation). This analogy, although quite simple, provides us with a direct and energetic picture of the essence of self-defence and lies at the origins of Taoism, Zen and authentic Kung Fu. In the same way as a flower, we cannot expect to express ourselves with power, authority and adaptability without a strong connection to the roots of self-defence. Expressing ourselves in life's battlefield becomes an insurmountable task without the support of our practise in Meditation, Chi Kung and Martial Science. The instinct of a flower is to turn its leaves and open to the sunlight, and martial artists must learn to turn and open themselves to any situation in the 'theatre of operations' of their lives.

The theatre of operations continually shifts and is one that you must define yourself through your awareness. For instance, barristers must learn how to express themselves whilst under pressure from judges, juries and clients, and doctors must learn to express themselves in the context of their practise or in an 'operating theatre'. The theatre of operations for martial artists is not only in physical combat situations but also in any area of their lives where imbalance is perceived. This perception or 'seeing' operates on many different levels. For example, the strengthening of awareness of our internal conversation can protect us against negative thought; awareness of our skeletal alignment can protect us against posture imbalances such as slouching; our Chi Kung training helps the body to destroy viruses before they imbalance our bodies, which will lead to the full-blown illness; Martial Science can make us become aware of a work colleague that is trying to undermine us; and our sense of distance can allow us to perceive an opponent coming towards us so that we can neutralize them by selecting the correct technique. This amounts to the practical application of holistic self-defence, the understanding of which is the key to Martial Art.

There are two ways that martial artists relate to conflict in their lives: first by dealing with situations that are beyond their control, such as being accosted in the street, and second by consciously challenging situations that are within their control, such as recurring fears. To deal with both of these the Three Stages of Combat (see page 229) and the Principle of Adaptability (see page 224) are essential. Situations that are beyond our control tend to happen instantaneously in the present moment without prior knowledge and include being mugged or receiving bad news. In such cases, there is very little time available for preparation and we must respond as the impression impacts upon our senses. On the other hand, there are situations where our awareness identifies an area where fear is operating, such as avoiding an oppressive work colleague, and we consciously decide to challenge it, perhaps because we have seen a tendency within ourselves to avoid conflict situations of this nature. In such situations, we have time to prepare and initiate a confrontation.

The defining criteria for a situation that we are not expecting is that we do not know the variables of when, where, who or how this situation will occur. By training in the core principles of Martial Art you will prepare yourself for the unexpected by developing your awareness and presence in a safe environment, such as your home or the 'dojo', in order that your skills are available to you in times of conflict. In order to illustrate this, imagine that you are going about your daily business when the phone rings, you pick up the receiver and hear the sound of your friend's voice and something in their voice alerts you at an unconscious level to an imbalance in their voice, something different in their normal homeostasis is communicated but it is not strong enough for your conscious mind to trust it. However, your friend then expresses to you via words some bad news that travels down the phone wires into your ears and is interpreted by the brain, which in turn elicits a reaction in your body. At this point your Martial Art training will enable you to ground the energy elicited by shock, allowing you to comprehend the situation clearly and apply a strategy to deal with the situation.

Situations that we bring about consciously because our awareness has identified an imbalance need to be approached in a slightly different manner. In such situations we work with our awareness to prepare for moments when they arise, such as a confrontation with a work colleague. We can prepare to be present and to bring our presence to bear so that under the pressure of 'combat' we can make a conscious decision in order to change, via our actions, the effect we have on the outside world. This sometimes means that the homeostasis of our life will be disturbed for an indefinite time, in which case the strength and stamina of our adaptability becomes a factor. Very often in cases where we need to challenge our life, our inner world reflects the outer; for example, perhaps we identify the sensation of fear within us when we fly and therefore make excuses and avoid the act of getting on an aeroplane in our outer life.

The correct attitude when training in Martial Art is of paramount importance if you wish to become more efficient in dealing with conflict in your life:

> The hardest thing in the world is to assume the mood of a warrior, it is of no use to be sad and complain and feel justified in doing so, believing that someone is always doing something to us. Nobody is doing anything to anybody, much less to a warrior.   Castaneda (1972)

We must therefore become aware again of the difference between martial sport and Martial Art. In martial sport, the 'end' or prize is often to achieve glory in the somewhat artificial setting of a tournament or the acquisition of a new colour of belt. That is not to say that participating in martial sport is useless for some valuable lessons may be learned in that 'theatre of operations'. Indeed, in martial sport you are often asked to express yourself in front of an audience and so will feel the effect of fear or nervousness in your body. But we must be under no illusion that our prowess in a tournament is a reflection of our effectiveness in life. No matter how you look at it, it is still an artificial situation, and the body knows it. On the other hand, the battles and challenges that your life throws at you are *real*. Very often, they will seem uncannily appropriate and it is sometimes said that God never gives us a challenge without the appropriate tools to meet it. One can begin to understand that most things that happen to us happen for a reason. We find that we continue to attract the same situations, the same types of people, the same relationships, the same feelings on Monday morning, and so on. Alternatively, we may carry with us a sense of unfulfilled dreams, reminders from our unconscious mind that there are more fulfilling things that we should be doing with our lives. Or there may be people who we would really wish to meet, but we cannot summon up the courage to create opportunities for this to happen. These are just a few of the types of battles we face. To study Martial Art just for the express purpose of winning trophies or as preparation for beating somebody up means that there will be a greater tendency to daydream and therefore not participate fully in the physical sensations available to you in the present moment. This will not only slow down the process of embodiment but will also drag you away from Martial Art into the realms of martial sport. This kind of desire obscures the true nature of Martial Art with an unhealthy wish to win. Even if we achieved our end and become a 'champion', this idea then becomes a very convenient image to hide behind. If this image becomes foremost in our mind when we are training then, as Bruce Lee says in the film *Enter The Dragon*, if we stare at the finger, we might miss all of 'the heavenly glory'. The key to Martial Art training is to focus your intent on the present moment and not primarily on the achievement of some external goal. It is only in the present moment that we can open to and receive the impressions that facilitate a connection and harmonization between our body, mind and spirit. This enables us to fight battles of a much more personal nature where, rather than dominating the situation immediately and becoming the victor, we accept that we are lacking and that certain parts of our being need to be developed. This is very different to indulging in negative thought or self-pity as instead we consciously challenge areas of our being that we do not wish to see and wage war on them so as not to make a decision out of fear but consciously out of our wish to evolve and ultimately to help our fellow man and the universe. Martial sport trivializes this aim into the ridiculous conquest of breaking boards, achieving trophies and impressing friends and the massaging of our already over-stimulated ego.

One way this challenging of the ego's appetite is traditionally brought about is in the practise of sparring. Sparring allows the Martial Art student to experience both of the aforementioned situations: the student must willingly spar with their teacher, Sifu or Master and must expect to go into this situation in order to experience themselves in a state of fear, uselessness and agitation in order to learn how they will react in a real situation. In correct sparring the Master should be able to provide the student with a controlled amount of pain and fear whilst at the same time being extremely attentive to the overall state of the student. Unfortunately, most martial sport training does not facilitate this kind of learning and sparring is reduced to a primitive pecking order, which is dominated by the most aggressive students. The correct attitude of sparring is more akin to musicians jamming together or following a conductor, where the goal is for both parties to learn and understand.

In conclusion, there are three topics that need consideration for the correct understanding of Martial Art: the Principle of Adaptation, the Three Stages of Combat and the application of exercises that are relevant to one's life on all levels.

adaptability

Adaptations means not clinging to fixed methods,
but changing appropriately according to events,
acting as is suitable.   **Zhang Yu (Sun Tzu 600 BC)**

Adaptations are made on the spot as
appropriate, and cannot be fixed in advance.

Jia Lin (Sun Tzu 600 BC)

To fit in with an opponent one needs direct
perception.   **Lee (1975)**

'The survival of the fittest' is a popular phrase that we have all heard
and it tends to be used in all kinds of contexts, from business to sport.
The common understanding of this phrase is that only the strongest
and most aggressive survive, but this is actually a misconception. The
term was first coined by Charles Darwin in *On the Origin of Species*
(1859) and then Herbert Spencer in *Principles of Biology* (1864–7).
Spencer used the word 'fittest' in the sense of the most suitable; he
was referring to the adaptability of animals to an environment, in other

words, the most able to 'fit in'. This is an extremely important difference in meaning and points to the concept of adaptability that lies at the very heart of Martial Art.

What Herbert Spencer was saying was that only life forms that develop the ability to adapt to their environment survive. So too with the martial artist. We have already defined awareness as the first line of defence. This awareness is clearly seen when a rabbit uses its highly evolved aural sense to pinpoint the sound of approaching danger. Presence is the second line of defence – it allows us to stand in front of a direct threat and remain centred. This skill can be seen in cats as they prepare for a fight by lowering their centre of gravity, pinning their ears back, raising their fur and eliciting sounds of combat. Both of these skills are fundamental to your ability to adapt. The centring process allows humans to hold their form so that they do not suffer the debilitating effects of the inevitable, nor the powerful reactions that occur from the fight-or-flight response. Centring utilizes a recurring theme in Taoism and Kung Fu training, summed up by the phrase 'empty in order to be full'. It describes a state of readiness wherein the quieter and emptier you are inside (free from internal conversation, tension, emotional agitation, etc.), the more able you are to perceive your opponent's movements and intentions. An opponent's movements, as learned in the Strategy of Distance and Strategy of Pressure sections, are what we use to trigger the appropriate self-defence technique. In essence, our techniques adapt themselves to our opponent's intentions; thus when utilizing the Strategy of Distance, for example, we do not try and strike with a punch when our opponent is still at Kicking Distance, but instead we allow our opponent's moves to dictate our use of the more appropriate Front Kick. In other words, we harmonize our movements with our opponent's, becoming 'one' with them. As Bruce Lee stated:

> The important thing is not to attempt to control the attack by resisting it with force (either physical or mental), but rather to control it by going with it, thus not asserting oneself against nature. All these are simply based on the harmonious interchanging of the theory of yin/yang. As long as we plan our actions, we are still using strength and will not be able to feel our opponent's movements, thus failing to comprehend the true application of yin and yang. In view of this, the two practitioners are actually two halves of one whole ...   **Lee (1975)**

Martial artists who have developed the ability to adapt do not try to meet force with either physical or mental force with the end result of dominating an opponent at the forefront of their minds, but in fact cultivate the attitude of harmonizing and adapting themselves to an opponent's movements in the present moment. In this way we can see the correct interpretation of the term 'survival of the fittest' directly mirrored in true Martial Art, and this is a key area where Martial Art and martial sport part company.

The deeper you go into Martial Art training the more this principle will become clear. In the Strategy of Pressure section we learned that as our opponent expands we contract and as our opponent contracts we expand, and this is the underlying principle behind adaptability to all our opponent's movements. If you learn to 'listen' and gather information about this underlying movement, your hands will learn quickly to adapt to your opponent.

The only place that adaptability can truly occur is in the present moment as it is only in the present that you can receive the subtle clues and 'telegraphs' that your opponent will give you as to their intentions. If you try to engage the assailant with a predetermined game plan or an overly aggressive or overly passive attitude then your sensitivity to the information available in the present moment will be greatly decreased.

Adaptability does not mean formlessness or being passive, quite the contrary in fact because in order to adapt you must have impeccable form and a tremendous inner activation. These are the core principles (roots and stem) that are developed in Meditation, Chi Kung and Martial Science. You must first have inner form so that reaction does not pull you out of form, you must then have learned how to simultaneously move and keep your form and you must have studied the language of body mechanics in order to apply the most efficient form of attack or counterattack. At the appropriate moment, we start to reverse the energy flow and this is also a process of adaptability and harmonization. Our opponent will have sent energy towards us via words, gestures, emotional energy or actual physical attack, and we could say that this form of behaviour is Yang and that through adaptability we become Yin so once again forming the famous Yin/Yang sign. Gradually, as we apply our techniques, we reverse the energy flow by sending it back into the opponent. Eventually the attack stops and so we have harmonized the situation.

Applying the Principle of Adaptability in life is an art that can transform many of our relationships and other areas where we find ourselves trapped in familiar cycles. We need to come into the present moment, open to our fears and then engage in the process of, if you like, human evolution. Next time you find yourself in front of a problem or a difficult person try to use Meditation to open to them and receive the vibrations that they emanate. This is gathering information not only about them (external) but also about your own reaction to them (internal). When talking to people try to listen carefully to one's own internal conversation that is usually always going on, and resist temptation to speak from association. Try to be in the present moment when you manifest with voice, gesture or facial expression, and try to see what effect you have when the other person receives your manifestations.

the three stages of combat

There are three basic stages of combat that need to be defined: pre-conflict, immediate conflict and post-conflict. They form the process that is undergone when faced with any form of conflict situation.

1 ***Pre-conflict.*** *This deals mainly with awareness and presence. First, you become aware that something is amiss or bothering you; this might be a sense of uneasiness before a big interview, somebody staring at you in a bar or perhaps a rowdy group approaching you in a street, giving you the sense that there may be a possibility of direct conflict. At this point, your body will start to react and you will need to activate your presence by moving into your body and grounding the upward motion of energy. Your ability to do this is governed by how well you have studied and embodied Meditation and Chi Kung (see page 94). Perhaps the aggressor will move away or lose interest or perhaps you forget about the impending interview so that no conflict actually takes place in the end, but if not and, say, the aggressor begins to approach you, the reaction within yourself will intensify. This is where pre-conflict ends and immediate conflict begins.*

2 ***Immediate conflict.*** *This is when direct confrontation occurs,*

such as when the time of your big interview actually arrives or the aggressor confronts you directly. In the latter case, if the aggressor closes the distance between you then, with your presence, you must prepare for the possibility of attack by applying the Strategy of Distance and opening to your attacker's body language. If you have embodied this strategy then if your attacker physically tries to strike you, you will be able to respond with the appropriate technique without having to think about it. A conflict does not always escalate to physical violence, it could just be a verbal or emotional attack, but the immediate conflict procedure will take its course and come to some sort of conclusion, at which point immediate conflict passes into post-conflict. In our interview example, you must apply the relevant strategy, such as gaining knowledge of the company's background, dressing appropriately, and so on.

3 **Post-conflict.** This needs special attention, as we tend to underrate its significance. Following conflict situations you will still have many of the chemicals released through fear circulating in your system; essentially, you will still be in shock. This is an altered state of awareness and can greatly increase the chance of accidents or misjudgments post-conflict. For example, following a road-rage incident you will need to refocus quickly if you have to drive so as to avoid an accident, or if you are a nurse then you will need to get yourself back to normal so that you do not make a mistake and harm a patient, or you may have to give a detailed statement to the police and thus require a clear head. Another example is following a big interview when you will want to control the anxiety of waiting to hear whether you succeeded. Realizing that you are in an altered state is the first step to dealing with it, and it is at this point that you should apply your techniques for grounding

energy to bring yourself back into a more 'normal' or familiar
state of being. You will probably feel the after-effects for some
time – the conflict scene may replay repeatedly in your head or,
as is a very common reaction, you may berate yourself for not
having acted in a particular way (very common after
interviews). Not only is it dangerous to be unaware of the
effects of post-conflict, but you can also waste a tremendous
amount of energy if you do not help your body to return to its
normal state of homeostasis through your training.

The key to refocusing in post-conflict situations is the ability to
practise nonattachment to internal conversation/daydreaming
and build a strong connection with the breath. The
remembrance of the immediate conflict is most powerful
directly afterwards, when the natural chemicals in your system
power internal conversation and images. When you become
aware that you are replaying and commenting on the conflict in
your mind, activate your presence, remembering the third
dimension of centring (dropping down and letting go), which
pulls the energy away from the head, so weakening internal
conversation. Becoming aware of the breath is the most
powerful method for restoring homeostasis because it brings a
balance between the somatic and autonomic nervous systems,
thus reducing the circulating fight-or-flight chemicals.

By looking at conflict in three stages, we prepare ourselves to
deal with the inevitable effects of shock. We use our Martial Art
skills in all three areas to lessen the effects of shock and begin to
bring some order to one of the most powerful experiences a
human can have.

HOW DRUGS AFFECT AGGRESSORS

Drug abuse is the number one cause of violent attacks in society today. Drugs insidiously work their way into people's lives, gradually modifying their behavioural patterns. People who abuse drugs create a chemical imbalance in their bodies, which can induce them to be violent. Contrary to popular belief, drugs tend to make people more predictable rather than less because each drug puts its own particular stamp on the user. It is a good idea to familiarize yourself with some of the basic psychological characteristics and symptoms of drug abuse. Outlined below are the drugs that I have found have the largest propensity to lead to violent behaviour.

Alcohol

By far the worst drug operating in society is alcohol. Not only is it legal, socially acceptable and freely available to all income levels, it also travels under the banner of 'let's all have a jolly good time'. In my years as a bouncer, I have seen countless proceedings that started out as a good time that, as the night wore on, were brought lurching to their inevitable conclusion of ridiculous conflicts and fights by the destructive effects of alcohol. Alcohol decimates all relationships until only the user's relationship to the drug itself remains. It has the peculiar characteristic of being able to turn husband against wife, brother against sister and friend against friend – many of the people (both men and women) who have come to me for training did so because of alcoholic partners. Alcohol can also intensify the 'pack hunting' instinct in certain groups of people so we therefore need to study the effects of alcohol on both individuals and groups, separately.

The Individual

The main effects of alcohol on the individual are fairly well known: increased confidence, loss of co-ordination, slurred speech and mood swings. Alcohol creates a bubble around its user, making him feel courageous – someone who seems shy and well mannered when sober can become a loudmouthed lout when drunk. In terms of self-defence, it is important to burst that bubble so that the assailant begins to perceive the situation in a more sober manner. Inhibitions are one of the primary forces holding the social and moral fabric of society together – when these are removed, we see a breakdown of acceptable behaviour.

Groups

As mentioned earlier, the 'pack hunting' instinct is exacerbated by alcohol and therefore soccer hooligans, organized gangs and teenage groups must all be considered extremely dangerous when under the influence. Violent situations involving groups often occur when 'showing off' gets out of control and this is prevalent in one of the most dangerous groups on the street today: adolescent youths.

Cocaine

Until quite recently, the price of cocaine meant that it was only available to those with money. One of the most obnoxious groups of people that I have had to deal with in nightclubs is 'coked up' city traders, the majority of whom come from good homes and have had expensive educations. However, under the influence of cocaine (and often also champagne) their misplaced sense of superiority reduces them to aggressive behaviour. The 'high' that cocaine induces is that of extreme confidence, which usually leads to excited talking and animated body language. A rapid 'come down' follows, which is characterized by paranoia, a loss of focus, long periods of silence and a feeling of isolation. Try not to confront or argue with people when they are high and instead wait for the telltale signs of the 'come down' before engaging them.

Crack

Crack (a.k.a. Rocks) is an extremely powerful form of cocaine that is smoked and not snorted. It produces the same effects as regular cocaine but the highs and lows are much more intense. The paranoia factor is extremely dangerous because an innocent remark made to someone on crack can be misconstrued by the user as being a threat, which can lead to violent behaviour. Crack also creates peripheral violence in the form of stealing and mugging to feed the user's addiction. People on crack usually exhibit classic 'junkie' symptoms such as sweating, agitation and extreme pupillary reactions.

Heroin

Unlike crack users, heroin junkies are not usually violent when they are actually on the drug but can be violent out of desperation to get money to feed their habit. Junkies tend to have poor health so are not looking to engage in physical confrontation although a disturbing trend in muggings by heroin junkies is the use of hypodermic needles as weapons, often claiming they are infected. Generally, if confronted with this situation give the mugger your money as it is not worth taking any risks and the mugger will usually leave you alone afterwards.

The following are some exercises based on common experiences in daily life. As we have come to understand, for Martial Art to be effective it must be practised, honed and used in the battlefield of one's life. This is an essential part of the process because it completes the circle of receiving, reacting and expressing, as illustrated by the example of a musician whose long hours of practise culminate in a performance where they receive a response from the audience and modify their expression correspondingly. Becoming aware of areas in your life where fear and excitement operate and then bringing your presence to bear on such areas is far more than just an exercise – it is participation in the everpresent process of homeostasis. Our lives present us with many real opportunities for observing ourselves in a state of imbalance, and if we become aware of these events then we can equally observe ourselves returning to the balanced state. By conscious repetition of this process we gradually become skilful at rebalancing our body, mind and spirit. The exercises that follow are designed to be a starting point; they are based on my own experiences and are the ones that have found the most resonance in people whom I have trained. The events that affect us are many and varied – what is significant for one person can often be insignificant for another – but some events seem to affect the vast majority of us in a similar way. Some of the exercises deal with Yin reactions that involve a closing down of the awareness and a withdrawal inside the self, whilst others deal with Yang reactions such as 'blowing one's top' or getting overly excited. If you practise perceiving yourself in daily life then gradually you will save a tremendous amount of energy that can be used in the maintenance of your physical, mental and emotional health; the pursuit of clear, focused goals; and the caring for and maintenance of your sphere of influence. However, if your reaction to events is allowed to continue in the 'dark' then your energy will be drained gradually like a battery short circuit and you will not have enough energy for your immune system to work properly, for you to maintain correct posture and ultimately for you to maintain a healthy homeostasis. As we have seen, this will lead to disease and eventually, directly or indirectly, death. All of the following exercises use awareness and presence as their principal defence mechanisms; however, in each case I will emphasize certain aspects of our presence and perhaps give you certain techniques for dealing with a particular situation.

The exercises are divided into three sections:

1 *Exercises that deal directly with personal safety to protect you from common crimes and dangerous situations.*
2 *Exercises that deal with social/work situations to protect you from situations that arise during 'normal' social intercourse.*
3 *Exercises that deal directly with your relationship with your 'self' to protect you from negativity and self-destruction.*

1 personal safety

THE KEY EXERCISE

When you go to use a key, say, in your front door, your visual perception must narrow its focus to the hand guiding the key into the extremely small aperture that it needs to fit. There is a tendency at this point for your whole awareness to contract as you become engrossed in the manifestation of the technique of unlocking the door. This is an extremely common moment for someone to be mugged as not only is their awareness weak but they are also about to unlock the door for a would-be thief! To prevent this from occurring, practise keeping your awareness expanded as you put the key in the door, perhaps focusing this awareness behind you as practised in Meditation. Try not to lean towards the keyhole, keep a straight back, be aware of your breathing and breathe out as you push the key into the lock and turn it. The most difficult part of this exercise is using your peripheral awareness as you put the key in the lock; the aperture becomes your focus point, but remember to expand your peripheral vision directly to each side at the same time.

The Key Exercise is a simple exercise for strengthening peripheral awareness and protecting yourself from a common mugging situation. It can be practised using the door to your house or workplace, your car door (if your car is equipped with electronic locking then practise as you reach for the door handle), the boot of your car (especially whilst loading shopping in underground/badly lit car parks), your mailbox or your bicycle lock (especially at night). As a footnote to this, you should always know where your keys are so that you do not end up fumbling around looking for them (another time when our attention is taken). Do not walk down the street whilst looking for your keys and only take them out when you actually reach your door. If you feel that you are being followed, monitor the level of your body's reaction to fear because it will interfere with your ability to put the key in the door. If you have an extreme reaction in your body or the person is following closely, do not go to your door but walk with purpose, using a focus point and correct hearing, to a safe place such as a crowded street, a neighbour's house or a bar.

At the time of writing this exercise, the following account of a mugging appeared in a daily newspaper, as told by the 41-year-old victim, a female barrister:

> I turned into my garden and up the stairs to the front door. I put my robing bag on the step and I was getting my key out to open the door when I heard noises behind me and I immediately felt my handbag pulled from behind. I started to scream to stop them. I thought the noise would attract attention and make them run off. I was holding the bag and it did not occur to me to let go. When I didn't let go, they started to kick me and then the man punched me in the face with a closed fist on the bridge of my nose and that's when I went to the ground. **Keeley (2003: 8)**

USING CASH MACHINES SAFELY

The principles of the Key Exercise can equally be applied when using cash machines, where there are two basic kinds of attacks, usually involving multiple assailants:

1 *The assailant waits behind you, tries to see your pin number and then grabs your card; and*
2 *The assailant waits for you to enter your pin number then pushes you out of the way, or a number of them will hold you there.*

Your visual awareness will once again narrow when you read the screen and type in a pin number so you need to expand it behind you and subtly try to get a look at who is behind you in the queue; if you do not feel right about it then leave. Your cash card is the key to your bank account so be careful when you are opening the door to it.

HOW TO DEAL WITH DRUNKEN AND ABUSIVE PEOPLE ON PUBLIC TRANSPORT

Using public transport offers us many opportunities to observe others and ourselves, largely due to the fact that we are locked in a confined space with them and cannot leave this space except at designated times. Most people tend to reduce their personal-space requirements according to how crowded a train or bus gets, but unfortunately this usually means a simultaneous contraction of their awareness. Many of you will have experienced what happens when a drunken or abusive person enters into this equation – people look away, bury their heads in books and newspapers, stare at adverts or pretend they are asleep – and the abusive person tends to enjoy this feeling of power and continues to indulge him/herself.

This contraction of the awareness is a symptom of denial; the people in the immediate vicinity of the abuser simply want the situation to go away so they contract into themselves as a way of removing themselves from the situation. However, you cannot afford yourself the luxury of 'sticking your head in the sand'. I once witnessed an abusive woman on an underground train pick on a well-dressed businessman – she started from quite far away with insults about his upper-class demeanour and when he tried to ignore her she moved closer, taunting him until she was two inches away from his face. Still he tried to look away, so she bit him on the nose! This is one of the most extreme cases of denial I have ever come across. When you become aware of an abusive person in this kind of situation, you should immediately find a focus point and become aware of your breathing as this will help to stabilize your centre and stop the process of contraction. The focus point could be anything, perhaps a book you happen to be reading, an advertisement or somebody's shoes. Then, once you have stabilized yourself, open up your peripheral awareness and focus it on the abusive person. Monitor their movements and voice to ascertain the motivation for their abusiveness, for instance, whether they are drunk, junkies or mentally unstable, and glean what you can from their appearance. The use of peripheral awareness and a focus point is a form of camouflage; you appear to be acting like everyone else. If you become aware, via your sense of distance, that they are becoming a direct threat to you then try and manoeuvre your body subtly into a place where you could spring (assuming you are sitting down) into action, and use your body of attention to ascertain the appropriate self-defence to use should you need it. Try to avoid direct eye contact with the person unless their abusiveness is focused directly upon you or unless you would like to create the opportunity to practise some of your self-defence techniques!

The Intelligent Warrior

What To Do When Strangers Approach You in the Street

Strangers in the street approach us for many reasons, some innocent and some not. The important thing is to apply your self-defence skills immediately whilst discerning their true motivations. It is helpful to divide these situations into two categories:

1   Strangers who approach you when you are moving; and
2   Strangers who approach you when you are stationary.

If you are moving, you must decide whether to stop or not. Generally speaking, if you are walking in a crowded city then it is a good idea to be using a focus point. This way you can use your peripheral awareness to monitor people approaching, and if you get a bad feeling about someone or you have discerned quickly their motivations and you do not wish to stop, such as for people begging (this is not a poke at those in hardship but because many of the increasing numbers of beggars on the street are professionals), then it is best to keep walking, utilizing your focus point and peripheral awareness. If they verbally accost you then use as short an answer as possible, perhaps together with a small hand gesture. Follow them with your peripheral awareness as you walk by and train your ears on them as they pass behind you, and keep walking with purpose.

If you decide to stop when they approach you then assume the Trigger Position (this includes turning on your presence), unless you feel confident in your assessment of them as a non-threat. If there is more than one of them, you must focus on the one who is talking whilst keeping your peripheral awareness on the others. Be very aware of anyone trying to move behind you; if someone does then move back slightly in order to keep him or her in your awareness. Exercise caution if the person asks you questions as this is a common device used to distract the attention before striking – try to access your memory without looking up or down, which is not as easy as it first appears but is yet another place where your training in the focus point is extremely useful. Beware of anyone leading your focus by, say, asking the name of a building whilst pointing at it or asking you the time (in the latter case lift your watch up to your face so that you can still see them, rather than looking down at your wrist). Use your peripheral awareness to check possible escape routes such as crowded streets or bus stops and, when you disengage in the conversation, be attentive to the moment that your back is turned towards them by keeping your awareness focused backwards for a time.

If you are stationary when a stranger approaches and you immediately get a bad feeling about them then the first option is to immediately start moving, which has to be done when they are still quite far away. Perhaps walk in a perpendicular direction to their line of force, monitor them with your peripheral awareness to see if they radically change their direction. If you have remained stationary, assume the Trigger Position and manoeuvre yourself to keep as many escape routes as possible in view. If you feel uneasy about the situation, do not engage in conversation just make an excuse and leave. If you are quite desperate, try calling and waving to someone in the distance as if they were a friend that you have been waiting to meet as this will usually make your assailant turn for a second, which is enough time for you to move. You could even run after the person you hailed, explain the situation and ask them to walk a few blocks down the road with you.

Some general rules when walking in the street are:

1   *Do not engage in lengthy conversations with strangers;*

2 *Do not carry bags in your hands, use a backpack; and*

3 *Try not to walk and talk on a mobile phone at the same time.*

Engaging in lengthy conversations with strangers only increases the chances of an attack as very often an assailant will use a conversation to disarm you and then attack when your guard is down or to pick a fight, as happened to me one night. I was hailed from behind by a friendly voice, the person ran past and stopped in front of me. He then asked for a cigarette and when I told him that I did not smoke he said that he did not believe me and that I was 'taking the mickey' out of him. A second later he launched one of the most stupid attacks I have ever seen and was rewarded with a solid right-hand punch to the side of his head. I then decided to leave in a hurry as his mates who had been watching from a distance were approaching quickly.

Walking in the street holding bags is not a good habit for two reasons: firstly, it is bad for your skeletal alignment; secondly, it ties up your hands and muggers will very often choose people who have both hands full. Use a backpack if possible as this remedies both of these situations.

Talking on a mobile phone in the street whilst walking is a dangerous proposition because when you talk to somebody on the phone you immediately project the body of attention to a different place such as the person you are talking to or the situation you are talking about. I have lost count of the number of times that I have been driving through busy streets when somebody has walked out in front of me, talking on a mobile phone. It also gives pickpockets more of a chance to succeed, and gives 'grab and dash' thieves a direct target (mobile-phone theft is one of the fastest-growing crimes). A female student of mine was sitting outside a café in Paris having a coffee whilst talking to a friend on her mobile phone; her table was near the side of a small road, and a thief rode by on a moped and grabbed her phone whilst passing by. In the process, the thief also grabbed some of her hair and yanked her clean out of her seat causing injury!

Another common time to be attacked in the street is when it is raining. Generally, when people walk in the rain they do not want to be so there is a tendency for them to imagine being somewhere else. This, combined with the wearing of hoods, the use of umbrellas, the change in acoustics due to the falling rain and the tendency to tense against the weather and look down, decreases people's general level of awareness. When walking in the rain try to use the awareness of your alignment to keep upright, and avoid wearing hoods as they dampen hearing, make it easier for muggers and pickpockets to approach you and decrease your awareness of approaching vehicles.

WHAT TO DO WHEN YOU ARE BEING FOLLOWED

The difficulty when you are being followed or feel like you are being followed is that you cannot use your vision to continually monitor a suspected assailant; this situation tends to increase panic in the same way that darkness makes us more afraid. It is crucial that you take a proactive attitude to being followed and if you can consciously centre yourself so that panic does not run riot it is possible to apply some strategy to the situation. Here are a few suggestions to help:

1   *Use your hearing developed in Meditation to focus on the sound of a suspected assailant's footsteps – you should be able to judge the speed of their footsteps in relation to your own and get an idea if they are gaining on you (this is a good exercise to practise*

even if you do not think you are being followed). It is also possible to tell your opponent's type of shoe (hard or soft), approximate weight and length of stride, plus how many people are pursuing you. In addition, if somebody is simply walking behind you innocently they will tend to give you a wide berth, especially at night and on a deserted street. If you hear footsteps coming right up behind you, take evasive action. (If you are studying a martial art, make sure you have a technique for turning and facing an opponent; if not, come and see me.)

2 Become aware of your feet. You might laugh but becoming aware of your feet pulls your attention towards the ground and is one of the keys to controlling panic. Moreover, by becoming aware of your own feet you will become much more attuned to the sound and feeling of your pursuer's feet.

3 Pretend to look at something that you are passing in the street, for instance, a car or shop window and, as your head turns to look at the object, use your peripheral awareness to catch a glimpse of your pursuer.

4 Use your peripheral awareness to look at reflections in car and shop windows; as your pursuer gets closer, you should be able to monitor them.

5 Change your direction suddenly by, for example, crossing the street. If you feel confident then try to time the crossing with an approaching car so that your pursuer cannot follow you immediately.

PROTECTiNG YOURSELF FROM ROAD RAGE

Over the last 20 years, we have seen the rise of a new form of human aggression known commonly as road rage. Most of us who drive on busy roads have, at one time or another, been exposed to aggression from our fellow motorists and many of us have been gripped by this particular kind of madness and expressed aggression ourselves. Several characteristics distinguish road rage from other forms of aggression. Firstly, the moment someone gets into a car they are surrounded by a metal skin, which immediately changes their psychology – they feel protected and it is if the car has became another body for them. Secondly, they can see out from this body and control its limbs (tyres) by various connections (steering wheel, brake, and so on) and they can, to a degree, express themselves with their car's instruments (there is even a rudimentary form of facial and vocal expression in the form of the horn and flashing lights). They can also express themselves by the usual methods of facial expression, body language and voice, but all from the safety of their new metal body. Lastly, when people drive there is a tendency, especially in cities, to be in a hurry and this haste leads to emotional agitation, which leads to more haste which in turn leads to people making ridiculous decisions such as rushing to get through traffic lights, speeding and cutting margins between cars, pedestrians and cyclists. And all for what? To get to their destination 20 seconds earlier or to hurry only to wait at the next light.

The sense of safety that the metal skin provides gives people the confidence to attack and berate others at a level that they would never dare if they were face to face with them. This expression then gives rise to anger in another motorist and we soon have an escalating situation. The communication that goes on between cars is riddled with what is commonly called 'projection'. For example, perhaps we see a car moving extremely slowly in front of us and we immediately assume that the person is a dawdler and a fool so we start berating them. Perhaps honking our horn, we angrily move to overtake them and, as we pull up beside them, give them one of our best angry stares. However, the whole of our action is based on the assumption that we know the motivations of the person driving the other car. It might turn out that their car is malfunctioning, or they have only just started to drive, or perhaps they are slowing down to manoeuvre into a parking space, and so on. The combination of projection and the readiness to resort to anger can quite literally be deadly. An angry person expressing himself or herself through a 3-ton piece of metal is a very dangerous proposition; misjudgments in speed, manoeuvring and braking occur, sensitivity to the outside world is cut down and sooner or later somebody gets hurt. Also, there are times when anger reaches such a pitch that the drivers stop, get out of their cars and argue face to face, which often leads to vicious physical violence which in turn can lead to the death or serious maiming of one or more of the participants. What is particularly ridiculous about the situation is that it is often the result of a simple misunderstanding and the parties do not actually want to fight but cannot back down because the level of escalation has gone too far.

Understanding road rage in the way described above can help to protect us from both the Yin (being on the receiving end) and Yang (sending aggression to others) perspectives. When somebody sends you aggression, try not to be caught by it; instead, let it bounce off your window! Remember the action/reaction pattern and connect to the sensation of your hands on the steering wheel, your spine against the seat, and attack them with a wave and a smile or something similar. If you sense the reaction of fear in your body, use your Natural Breath Cycle *(see page XXX)* to regain your homeostasis as you do not want this reaction to cause an accident 50 yards down the road. Never get out of your car unless absolutely necessary or if you want to practise your self-defence techniques – remember what is at stake and that the situation can turn ugly in an instant. Whilst riding along the road recently I noticed the car in front going across the small roundabout and at that moment, a scooter cut in front of the car. The driver of the car immediately started honking his horn and angrily overtook the scooter and forced it to a stop by stopping at an angle in front of it and hence reducing the space between the car and the concrete reservation in the road's centre. The car driver got out of his car and started to yell abuse at the scooter driver; he was a well-built young man who obviously felt like he could handle himself in this situation. Unfortunately, the car driver had not realised that the scooter was travelling in a pack and soon found himself surrounded by an indignant mob of scooter-driving youths. It was obvious from his body language that the car driver was experiencing fear, yet at the same time he was trying to maintain the front of being a tough guy. The youths closed in around him and one of them gave him an exploratory shove whilst the others began to berate him. Still acting the tough guy, the car driver retreated a few feet to his open car door then got in and slammed the door shut. That might have been the end of it but he foolishly floored the accelerator, leaving the youths in a cloud of acrid burned rubber from his tyres. The youths gave chase and, unforeseen by the driver, 50 yards down the road the car had to stop in a queue of traffic. The youths caught up and started to smash his car up using their helmets, and this time the driver did not get out of his car and thought he was safe until a crash helmet smashed through the sunroof, cutting him badly. This is an excellent example of how some bad decisions taken in anger can escalate out of control. If you feel anger and indignation rising in your body and you are in danger of 'blowing your lid', try to remember what is at stake. Remember your overall focus and do not be pulled off course – it is not worth going to prison for or losing something that you truly value. Connect to your five points, breathe and in no time at all you will have forgotten all about the 'idiot' in the other vehicle.

CONTROLLING PANIC IN THE FACE OF AIR RAGE

Air rage is also escalating in our society. When people travel on planes there is always an underlying level of excitement and fear; the seasoned traveller is not affected as much as the annual holiday traveller but excitement and fear are usually always there to some degree or another. For this reason it is important to bear in mind the Action/Reaction Cycle for everyone will react slightly differently in airports and on planes than in their daily lives. People tend to become indignant quicker on planes, mostly because when they fly they feel slightly more important than usual and therefore there is a tendency to be more judgmental of others. The vast majority of air-rage incidents on planes involve alcohol consumption. Alcohol behaves slightly differently in the bloodstream because of the changing air pressure inherent in flying but unfortunately this simple fact is lost on most drinkers and hence they do not see the changes in their behaviour until it is too late. If you should come into proximity of overtly violent behaviour whilst flying, be aware that the tendency to panic will be much more likely in yourself and those around you. For this reason, if you have to deal with someone being aggressive then always allude to a higher power; for instance, remind them of the severe attitude that the police and judicial system will take to their behaviour.

USING NOISY NEIGHBOURS TO OBSERVE YOUR BOILING POINT

Noisy neighbours offer you a chance to observe the battle between action and non action that can rage within. This scenario also offers us a chance to observe our irritation and anger beginning to 'boil'. To start with, a noise that a neighbour is making will be simply irritating to us as we will tend to give them the benefit of the doubt and wait to see whether it disappears. However, if the noise continues then our anger will begin to grow and we will usually start to complain aloud to others or ourselves. At this point, we have the opportunity to see ourselves as we begin to be taken over by our anger. This is usually when internal conversation begins to weigh up the merits of various courses of action such as banging on the wall, calling the police, making a loud noise ourselves in retaliation or going next door and ringing their door bell. If you choose direct confrontation then do not go around to their door and scream at them, but control your anger and inform them of the problem (they may not even know they were disturbing you and be apologetic); you do not want to start a conflict where there does not need to be one. If they persist with the disturbance, then it is a good idea to use official channels such as the police or an environmental health officer to make them see sense before any further direct confrontation is initiated.

2 social

HOW TO CLAIM BACK PERSONAL SPACE FROM SPACE INVADERS

The invasion of someone's personal space is a little crime that happens all the time and is very often used for sexual or intimidating purposes. Most people feel comfortable with a personal space round them of approximately 36 inches, corresponding to the Auric Field, an electrical field that emanates from the physical body that has been part of Chinese medicine for over 3000 years and has recently been measured 'scientifically' by Western research. One of the most common times when this space is invaded is sexual harassment in the workplace; here, both men and women push the boundaries of what is acceptable for cheap thrills and sexual speculation. It is a tricky place to protect yourself because of the complex nature of relationships within a company, for instance, your boss has a certain power over your career and you have to work in harmony with fellow employees to get the job done. If you feel that your personal space is being invaded, try some of the following:

1. *Become aware of your spine – the common saying 'to stand up for yourself' has come about for a reason. A straight spine brings you up to your full height, gives you poise and stops you from cowering away from the situation, and has a tendency to elicit feelings of power and 'uprightness' in the body. Very often, someone who invades your personal space does so because they get a perverse pleasure in watching someone else cringe or contract away. By keeping a connection to your straight spine this pleasure will be denied them. It is important to remember not to hold your spine rigidly but to allow it to find its natural alignment – a rigid spine very often communicates fear, which for many 'invaders' is also a 'turn on'. The poise that is communicated through a correctly aligned spine can help you to very subtly project an aloofness or coldness to your assailant and this is the best attitude for dealing with the heat of someone's sexual advances as it is least likely to provide food for their misguided appetite. You can become aware of your spine in the sitting or standing position.*

2. *Use a gesture and a controlled voice if the person does not get the hint. Sexual harassment tends to live in dark corners, just below the level of perception of everyone else in the working environment. By using a gesture, you can draw attention to yourself and catch somebody's eye; a strong, slightly raised voice, perhaps saying 'please will you back off you are making me feel uncomfortable', also attracts attention. If you attract attention to the situation you make it clear to those around you what is going on and can quite easily embarrass your invader. If no one else is around it makes your position very clear so that no further indiscretions are likely to take place. Remember, training in Chi Kung strengthens the connection between breath and movement and this will allow your voice and gesture to act as one unit.*

3   *Know the correct channels of complaint so that you can use them as a threat. This weapon will also make you feel confident.*

4   *Use the Fence Position* (see page 199) *from Martial Science if the invader does not take no for an answer and continues to engage you.*

Defence against other forms of personal-space invasion is similar except that between two men the energy will probably be different than between a man and a woman as it tends to be far more combative and not so seductive (or sleazy). However, when invasion occurs in a non-aggressive situation such as in an elevator or on a crowded train then you need to focus more inwardly, connecting with your feet on the ground and most importantly the breath. Feel the space inside yourself, open with your peripheral awareness to the confines of three-dimensional space and feel the space that you are filling. In cramped situations, we tend to try to make ourselves smaller, which always involves tension in the body. Resist any temptation to engage in internal conversation, especially about what people think of you. Ironically, the way to feel more at home in a cramped environment is to open to it and sense the other people whilst keeping your internal connection. You will see that they are reacting and withdrawing inside themselves at which point *you* will command the three-dimensional space. When leaving a cramped environment, try to be present to the feelings of relief as they wash over your body. In this way you will get an impression of the whole process: the changes that occurred when you first moved into a small environment (pre-combat), you maintaining your equilibrium (immediate combat) in the environment and you leaving the situation and its immediate effects receding into the background (post-conflict). This type of understanding could be applied to any of the exercises in this section.

There are times in our lives where we have to stand in front of people who are verbally abusing us, such as strangers, friends, work colleagues or partners. The old saying 'sticks and stones may break my bones but names will never hurt me' is only true if you do not allow the names to hurt you. I have had people come to me who have endured years of verbal abuse, and the detrimental effect on their homeostasis is very real, believe me. Being hit by verbal energy is no different to being hit physically although the effects take longer to show themselves – spinal alignment tends to go as the person feels more and more 'downtrodden' and self-esteem plummets; nervous problems appear such as tense facial masks, mumbling, difficulty in focusing the eyes due to years of avoiding somebody's gaze, and so on. The danger of continual verbal abuse is that it regularly pushes the body out of the state of homeostasis; therefore, if it is left unchecked it will cause disease in the body.

There are also one-off incidents of verbal abuse, such as road rage, which are usually of an extremely intense nature. A stranger very often perpetrates this kind of abuse but it is also very common in the workplace. In terms of self-defence, this type of abuse is dangerous because it can literally freeze the body when it enters, rendering technique useless. The human voice is an extremely powerful instrument that embodies physical (volume), mental (the meaning of the words being spoken) and emotional (pitch, rhythm and intensity) power and therefore it hits us on different levels simultaneously and the body simply cannot cope with the shock. It is important to apply the principles of nonattachment outlined earlier in the book and here are some further suggestions on how to deal with the situation:

1. **Connect to your hearing.** This is where verbal abuse enters the body; try to hear it not as somebody abusing you but as a strange kind of music that has rhythm, pitch and phrasing. This will lessen the personal shock that you will experience and facilitate the next point. Remembering this lessens energy of the abuse on impact.

2. **Connect to your feet on the ground.** This pulls the energy entering the ears down through the body and literally grounds it much like an electrical circuit. An intense verbal attack is like an electric shock – it can 'fry' your nervous system or you can use the nervous system to channel the energy to the ground.

3. **Utilize your deep breathing.** This is extremely useful for maintaining your emotional equilibrium as there will be a strong tendency for you to have a Yin (such as crying or taking subservient postures) or Yang (such as yelling back or escalating the wounding capacity of your insults) reaction to verbal abuse.

4. **Keep your face relaxed.** Due to the fact that most people contort their face when they use physical abuse, it is helpful to keep one's own face relaxed as this allows you to sense your abuser's face and practise nonattachment. The recognition of facial expressions is of profound significance for human communication (there is a part of the brain that deals exclusively with this recognition); therefore, when an aggressive expression is received through the eyes it carries a strong charge. Partners?

5. **Use positive nonverbal affirmations.** Showing the person you are listening to them by nodding your head occasionally or using an 'uh-huh' is an excellent way to defuse a situation because it allows you to organize your own thoughts clearly and carefully whilst appearing to be completely involved in the person's tirade.

The last point is extremely useful in personal relationships because very often our partners are looking for a certain emotional reaction from us when they get upset. If you begin to become more centred and calm in front of them it can sometimes make them even angrier, but using small nonverbal affirmations can reassure them that you are paying attention to them. Bringing your presence to bear can very often be excellent 'medicine' for flash points in a relationship as if you continue to be present then very often your partner will follow suit and not be so susceptible to 'flying off the handle'. In addition, in personal relationships you must always be aware that there is a great tendency for verbal abuse and arguments to ensue after the consumption of alcohol, the most effective drug for destroying loving relationships. Keeping this in mind can help you to keep an objective viewpoint on the situation and will alert you to the stages of alcoholism in yourself, your partner or other loved ones.

If the intensity of the verbal abuse increases to the point where you sense it might become physical then assume the Trigger Position and be prepared to apply the Fence Position if they start to get right up 'in your face'.

Standing in front of verbal abuse is quite a complex situation because there are so many permutations that can occur. The points outlined above may seem like quite a lot to remember but if you have practised Meditation and Chi Kung then you should be able to access them simultaneously. Following is an exercise to help you with this.

CONSCiOUSLY STANDiNG NEAR VERBAL ABUSE

There will be times when we witness other people verbally abusing each other. When this happens, go and stand at a sensible distance from the situation, pretend to be waiting or reading, then consciously open to their exchange by using peripheral awareness and sending your body of attention to the situation. You are likely to begin to feel the effects of fear in your body but to a much milder degree than if it was you in the situation. You can then apply some of the techniques from the last exercise and hence gain valuable experience in a real situation. This can be applied to any conflict situation or form of abuse that you witness: road rage, disgruntled customers in shops or an actual street fight.

Using Simple Money Transactions to Overcome Shyness

This is an excellent exercise for strengthening your presence in front of strangers. I highly recommend this exercise to anyone who feels that they suffer from shyness and/or fear of meeting new people.

When you enter a shop to buy something you have to come face to face and interact with a stranger behind the till. Bring your presence to bear on the situation, say 'hello' directly to them and observe without judgment their reaction. Which way does their energy flow? How does their body change shape? Try to be present all the time when they are ringing up your items, use your peripheral awareness to observe their movements and notice the way that they tell you how much money you owe. There is very often a feeling of pressure, especially if there is a queue, to get your money out quickly (remember the maths professor?) but try to relax. Most importantly, be present for the moment when money is transferred, when your hand will probably touch the other person's, which can also happen if you receive change (this process is the same if you are using a credit card). Finally, be attentive to how many times they say 'thank you' and 'goodbye' and try to look them in the eye and say 'thank you' once and 'goodbye' once. By practising this exercise, you will gain valuable experience in opening to and observing strangers and you will begin to sense when they are present and when they are not; you will also sense the habitual nature of their movements and interactions when in front of a customer. The moment when money is transferred is significant because you both reach out and must communicate on a physical level, whilst controlling your greeting, thanks and goodbyes allows you to shape your energy into a clear expression in front of a stranger.

Surviving Those Difficult Phone Calls or Meetings of an Emotional Nature

I am sure that you can recall a time when you have had to make a difficult phone call or meet with somebody of an emotional nature, for instance, when breaking up with a partner or firing somebody, and it is helpful to apply our three stages of combat to such situations. To start with there is usually an apprehension or resistance before the meeting (pre-combat), then there is the actual communication (immediate combat) followed by the 'come down' (post-combat). Try to be aware of the feelings of resistance and apprehension in the body, perhaps you put off making the phone call or you experience feelings of fear as you enter the place of your meeting. Try to focus clearly on what it is you want from the situation – as Bruce Lee said, 'if you don't aim at something you are not going to hit it' – and be prepared for the other person to argue and try to change your wishes. During the communication try to bring your presence to bear and, as it is an emotionally charged situation, stay connected to your deep breathing. Place special awareness on the moment that you express your wishes and open to the effect that your words have on the other person. Afterwards you must try not to engage in internal conversation or replay the meeting in your imagination. A good way to help you come down afterwards is to slowly practise some of your Chi Kung exercises or go for a walk using your focus point and connection to the five points of co-ordination.

You can also apply this strategy when asking someone for something that you want, such as a date or a job.

Walking into Unknown Environments without Shrinking

When we walk into a crowded place for the first time it is quite common to experience varying degrees of fear in the body. A symptom of this is contracting our awareness when we try to make ourselves as small as possible so as not to attract attention. If the crowded place is a bar then the situation is often exacerbated by the overconfidence brought on by the consumption of alcohol, for instance, men under the influence are not so afraid to stare a bit longer at a woman who enters by herself. The strategy for dealing with this kind of situation is very similar to the strategy for claiming your personal space in that you must bring the attention into your body and be aware of the space inside (breathing can help here because it fills an inner space), which stops the movement of contraction. Then expand your awareness outwards (connect to the spine) and scan the room slowly as if you were looking for somebody but in reality use your peripheral awareness to feel the space of the bar and the fact that it is just a shell with some tables, chairs and people in it. Every now and again, look specifically at a group of people and notice where their attention is directed (part of you will be relieved to find out that they are not all looking at you critically!). This process need only take 10 seconds; consciously repeating it over a period of time can help tremendously in our self-confidence when meeting groups of new people, for instance, when walking into a new workplace on your first day.

Dealings with the Police and Other Figures of Authority

The police have a way of 'striking fear into people's hearts' – it is one of the primary tools that makes them effective. Most of us will be able to recall a time when we felt the reaction of fear when pulled over for a traffic offence or stopped in the street, and for this reason take the opportunity to work with your presence and consciously relax when in communication with them. Try to see the person behind the uniform or the badge; relax when their attention is turned away from you, for instance, when they are writing a ticket or talking on the radio; and be aware of feelings of self-consciousness when passers-by look at you. To a lesser degree, you can work in this way with customs officials, tax inspectors, unexpected speed cameras and traffic wardens, though in the case of the latter because the uniform does not carry the same authority you might have to work to ground your expressions of anger and indignation!

Doctors, Dentists and Dealing with Pain

The offices of doctors and dentists are excellent places to observe fear in the body because visits to both often involve the expectancy of pain. In addition, when we visit the doctor we are often worried that something is wrong with our health and we start imagining all kinds of terrible diagnoses (most people suffer from a mild form of hypochondria); here we must gain control of our imagination and the pictures of death and suffering that it tends to throw up. Some of you may have had to wait for results of tests, which can be an incredibly anxious time and cause your symptoms to get worse; in times like these you must practise Meditation and Chi Kung more often. If you have a specific health complaint then whilst Defining the Body open to the area in order to actively participate in the healing process.

Going to the dentist creates a fairly opportunity where we are going to allow someone to hurt us! Although in this day and age pain is greatly reduced by anaesthetic, there is still usually some form of pain and discomfort. Try to be aware of the tension that creeps into the body as the dentist goes to work; consciously relax the body via the breathing and feel by doing this that you are working *with* your dentist to fix your teeth. It is an excellent opportunity to watch the battle between tension and relaxation and you must continually monitor the battle in order to maintain relaxation of your body. One of the reasons for this is that we generally lie down in a dentist's chair and because we are horizontal more energy is available to us – it is nature's healing 'posture' and when we are very ill we instinctively return to it. Practising connection with the five points of co-ordination can replace our normal grounding process and help to draw the energy away from the expected point of pain; this is traditionally how the control of pain was taught in Kung Fu schools. Pain, like everything else in the body, takes energy so if you pull the energy away from the pain then the pain lessens. This is why the expectancy of pain usually increases the amount of pain perceived. Another form of pain control comes by consciously projecting your body of attention to another place, say, relaxing on the beach. This confuses the subconscious mind, which, as it does not know which one is reality, splits the energy into both. Masters of pain control can usually completely stop the messages of pain from reaching the brain; it is also possible to do this under hypnosis or with acupuncture. Your first step to achieving a degree of pain control begins in the process of Meditation – remember that the skill of directing and shaping the body of attention lies behind all other skills.

How to Apply Your Presence in Meetings

Meetings or gatherings with two or more people are always an interesting challenge for the Intelligent Warrior as you must hold more than one person in your awareness and simultaneously sense when you need to speak (Yang) and when to be quiet (Yin). Speaking too loudly, too frequently or out of turn will make people resent and ignore you whereas not speaking enough or clearly will make people think that you are not interested or that you have nothing of importance to contribute. This may seem obvious, but striking a balance between the two can be tricky, especially during an important or highly charged encounter.

In order to become aware of everyone simultaneously you must activate your state of awareness that you built during your training. This will allow you first to find your centre and claim your personal space and then to utilize your peripheral awareness (especially the sight and hearing) to listen to the current speaker whilst also sensing the reactions of the other people in the room to the speaker's comments. For this I would recommend that you find a focus point that allows you to view as many people as possible and your use of it should be fairly well disguised, for instance, pretend to look at your notes or the flower arrangement in the middle of the table. You must focus your hearing on the speaker in order to follow their logic but if you have trained correctly, you should have enough attention to simultaneously sense the other listeners in the room. To start out with become aware of their body language and frequency of fidgeting and making gestures. In terms of your participation in the meeting, if you find it hard to speak up then try using small verbal affirmations, such as 'mm mm' or 'I see', or perhaps ask a simple question. This will bring your attention up into your vocalizing machinery (in essence, warming it up) and help you get over the inertia of hesitation. If you are the type of person who talks too much and gives yourself away then connect to your breathing and the impression of your tongue touching the hard palate behind the teeth; if you feel an impulse arising in you to speak then resist it and listen closer to what is being said. If you can do this then very often the content of your original impulse will evolve into something of greater weight and insight, or you will sense that it was actually not worth saying.

These simple and direct techniques can help transform your effectiveness in meetings by allowing you to strengthen your presence without becoming aggressive.

Action or Nonaction: Dealing with People who Jump Queues

People who push in front of you in queues sometimes offer us an excellent opportunity to study the dilemma of action or nonaction. When we perceive somebody pushing in front of us it can often trigger indignation followed by a fairly intense internal conversation about whether or not to tell the person to get to the back of the queue or say that you were there first. This situation is interesting because you can observe one part of yourself wishing to act (Yang) whilst another part hesitates (Yin) and inhibits action, usually utilizing elaborate excuses to justify your nonaction. This interplay of opposites is the most valuable experience in this situation, whether you act or not is secondary. In situations like these always remember your overall goals, for instance, is telling someone to get to the back of the queue and perhaps provoking a confrontation which could escalate what you really need on the way to, say, a big interview or the airport? On the other hand, perhaps you noticed that you do not stand up to people as much as you could and so here is an excellent opportunity to practise and gain experience of this. Very often, our ego gets involved in situations like this — it feels indignant then creates excuses to justify action to preserve the image you have of yourself. It is also extremely interesting in such situations to observe others engaging in the battle between action and nonaction.

You can easily apply your experience of this scenario to other situations such as telling someone not to smoke on a train or when someone steals your parking space.

Overcoming Resistance to Asking for What You Want

Another place to observe the above-mentioned battle is when you have to ask for something you want such as a pay rise, promotion, favour or date. These situations tend to elicit internal conversation about action or nonaction and offer an additional chance to observe ourselves. When we wish to ask somebody for something we often prepare by consciously or unconsciously imagining ourselves asking for it. We might feel courageous and confident in our imaginings so full of optimism we then set off to meet the person. However, the moment we get in close proximity to the person or the time for the meeting draws near, the fight-or-flight response triggers, we begin to feel nervous and there is a tangible resistance to expressing our request. This resistance is very often enough for our internal conversation to start making excuses for why we do not have to make our request today! Of course, this type of reaction varies from person to person but it is usually present to some degree or another. When you become aware of the resistance within you, become aware of your breathing (remember the common advice of taking a few deep breaths before an important event), accept the fear and resistance in your body, recall why you are doing this in the first place and then carry out your request. After the event, continue to observe the reaction in your body, the tone of which will depend on whether you judge the outcome as a positive or negative. Do remember though that each outcome brings a different experience for you to learn from (see *How to Unlock the Wisdom of Our Mistakes*, page 274).

Protect Yourself from the 'Blow' of Bad News

Recall a time when you received some bad news, how one second everything was fine and then the next your whole inner and outer states had changed. These situations are very similar to conflict situations in that there are basically two ways we can receive bad news:

1   *The news strikes us 'out of the blue' (for instance, on hearing that a friend has been in a car crash).*
2   *We have time to prepare for the possibility of bad news (for instance, sitting in a doctor's surgery waiting for the results of a test).*

In both cases it is helpful to remember that after the brain receives the news via the senses and interprets the message there follows a chemical reaction in the body (very often comprising an intense reaction in the solar plexus, an increased heart rate and feeling flushed). Because of this reaction, an intense internal conversation follows.

Receiving bad news is a form of pain and hence we can apply some of the same principles to it that we would to controlling physical pain. Controlling pain always involves directing your attention away from the area of pain and into your whole body in order to both lessen the pain and slow down the internal conversation that tends to make us panic or think that the pain is worse than it really is. In terms of bad news, this can help to clear your mind so that you can apply a strategy for regaining your homeostasis after this 'blow'.

3 your 'self'

UTILIZING CLOSE CALLS TO YOUR ADVANTAGE

All of us at some time or another in our lives have close calls that trigger the effects of fear in the body, for instance, a near miss whilst driving, walking out in front of a car, nearly coming off a bike or falling down the stairs. In these situations, your body will receive an instantaneous adrenalin hit, which you can use to gain valuable experience of being in a real state of fear. One of the most noticeable symptoms will be your heart starting to beat faster and harder. Open to this sensation and at the same time become aware of your deep breathing; try to stay with the sensation as your heartbeat returns to its normal homeostasis whilst continuing with whatever task you were performing at the time. This is excellent for keeping you moving in times of fear. The energy that is released in the body will also have a tendency to make internal conversation more intense but try not to engage in it.

These actions can also be applied to any situation that the mind recognizes as a close call when perhaps it is not, for instance, the fear of flying or watching a scary movie. Part of our mind does not recognize the difference between what is reality and what is not but we can use these moments just as well to benefit our understanding.

The Art of Waiting

Waiting is something that we all have to do at various times; it is an opportunity to integrate the physical body with the body of attention. Whilst waiting there is a very great tendency for people to project into the future and think about where they are going or wish for the train to arrive or the light to turn green. Both Taoist and Zen writings are full of stories about the benefits of learning to wait patiently. When you are in a situation where you have to wait, try to come strongly into your body and receive impressions of what is happening now in the present moment and remind yourself that there is absolutely nothing you can do to make the train or bus arrive quicker. Accept the wait and enjoy the incredible array of impressions available to you at that moment. Find a focus point and practise your peripheral awareness; try to use it to see the train coming or the light turning green. If you are waiting with others then try to sense their agitation, for instance, they might be continually staring down the road looking for a bus, and you will convince yourself of the absolute futility and the incredible amount of wasted energy that comes from 'fighting' moments when we are forced to wait. Gaining this kind of perspective in your life will make you realize that any situation, good or bad, can be turned into positive work for strengthening your homeostasis.

Learning how to wait correctly is also a tremendous self-defence skill, as many attacks occur at late-night taxi ranks and bus stops. When waiting in these situations stand so that a wall or bus shelter protects your back, find a focus point and open up your peripheral awareness so that you can see everyone in your view. In this way, you will become aware at an early stage of any potential attackers.

How to Defend Against Unexpected Bills

You wake up in the morning refreshed and invigorated, ready to take on a new and wonderful day. You walk past your front door and see the mail awaiting you on your doormat. As you pick up your mail expecting a nice letter from a friend, an official-looking envelope catches your eye and tension begins to creep into you body. Horror of horrors, it is a huge bill! All of a sudden, your world changes and images of lack and impotence creep into your mind. It is time to defend yourself! For those of you who are not millionaires, the fragility of one's cash flow is a constant source of fear. Money is one of the things that directly cuts into our sense of homeostasis because a large part of our lifestyle or status quo is maintained by it and our imaginations are often assailed by images of destitution. True security lies not in the knowledge that you will always have money but that you can actually survive without it. In the case of the unexpected bill, try to remember how you felt before you opened the envelope and how you felt afterwards – this is an excellent opportunity to see how our inner state changes our perception of our world. To combat the effect of this kind of shock bring your presence to bear, paying special attention to any tightening in the solar plexus region, then using your head apply a strategy for dealing with the situation. Emotional reaction and money do not mix very well (as any good stock trader will tell you), so your first job is to channel the fear away from your head so that you can get to work on a solution. You can apply this strategy whenever you have a financial mishap, for instance, when you receive a parking ticket or repair bill or you lose some money.

How to Unleash the Performer in You

The whole question of performance is interesting and is one that I have alluded to at various points in this book. Here we will look at performance in the normal sense of the word, as in some form of entertainment, and not as in how well you perform when somebody is trying to 'knock your block off'. Performance brings the whole question of the ego into our study for it is the ego that fears its own death when you walk on stage and it is because of this that the body feels threatened and starts to fire, in varying degrees, its survival reactions, which we have come to know as the fight-or-flight response. The performance could be to three or four people or to three or four thousand people, it does not really matter to the ego; it may be a performance of music, drama, comedy, dance, or it may be a presentation to your fellow colleagues. The fact of the matter is that you will walk out onto a platform and the attention of your fellow human beings will be directly focused upon you. Depending on your experience and the type of person that you are, you will either thrive on this to the point of addiction or fear it more than death itself. Both of these reactions need to be viewed objectively. The essence of performance is communication with your audience and this must be paramount in your mind at all times – if you are overconfident then you will be in danger of embarking on an 'ego trip' and if you are lacking in confidence then the message that you are trying to impart will be impaired by your nervousness. When we walk on stage and the attention of the audience is focused upon us we perceive a force coming towards us and the intensity of this force depends on the energy contained in it and the ground that it lands on (the level of intensity can be the same for a person performing to two people and a dog and a person performing to 5,000 people in Las Vegas).

Again our three stages of combat come in useful: when preparing to go on stage find your deep breathing and enter into your body and keep in mind the message that you wish to impart (remember, if you do not aim at something you will probably not hit it) – sometimes, whether you are religious or not, it a good idea to entreat some higher power in the form of prayer to help you increase your presence at the exact moment that you walk on stage (pre-conflict). Your performance on stage depends on how deeply you have embodied your particular skill at the moment of performance – this is not a time for thinking in the normal way but is a time for acting and reacting to your audience (immediate conflict). After your performance you will have to deal with the energy that will remain inside your body and the increased attention that other people will focus upon you – you should 'keep your feet on the ground', especially if you have performed well, and if you think that you performed badly then you will also have to defend yourself against feelings of negativity powered by the adrenalin rush of being on stage (post-conflict). If you look at performance in terms of this process, you will be in less danger of terminating your wish to express yourself because of perceived negative feedback or of 'acquiring a big head'. Performing can be a life-enhancing activity and one that many people deep down wish to achieve so regardless of the outcome, you should give yourself a pat on the back for 'getting up there' and doing it.

The Loss of Keys, Wallets and Other Precious items

The next time that you misplace or lose your keys or wallet/purse, try to see the effect that it has on you. Almost immediately pictures of inconvenience (cancelling credit cards, not being able to get into your house, being late for an important meeting) will appear in your imagination and voices in your head will tell you how you do not deserve this or how stupid you are. You will slowly work yourself up into such a frenzy that you will not even see just in front of your eyes where your wallet is lying.

These situations offer an excellent opportunity to see how easily we are dis-integrated, to the point where we do not trust our own eyes and repeatedly go back and look in the same places. You will also be able to experience the increase of the intensity of frustration that attacks us at times like these. You have therefore been presented with the opportunity to see yourself and gradually practise bringing some integration back into your life.

In these situations, it is essential that you clear your mind so that your subconscious can suggest where the lost item might be and you can connect with the sight and look carefully, with confidence, for the item. In order to clear your mind quickly, stop the body moving, close your eyes to refresh them, connect to the sensation of the feet and the breath, give yourself a certain number of breaths to stay motionless (five is a good number) and then re-enter the battlefield. The most important thing about this situation is that you see yourself. If the loss is genuine or you have been robbed, then clearing your head will allow you to apply a strategy that will limit the damage, for example, cancelling credit cards or calling a locksmith.

Procrastination: a Dangerous Adversary

Procrastination is another common occurrence in life where we can see the warring sides of ourselves. A good example is the resistance to menial tasks such as washing the dishes, organizing one's desk or folding the laundry. The funny thing about these situations is that we often spend far more energy avoiding a task than it would actually take to do it in the first place. One side of us says, 'we should do the dishes' whilst the other side starts to make excuses for not doing the task and, with immaculate creativity, starts to find all kinds of diversionary tactics. We can look at this in quite a light-hearted way but the truth of the matter is that we actually waste an incredible amount of time in procrastination, the cost of which is very often that we never achieve what it is we really want to do. By recognizing the mechanics of procrastination in small, simple tasks you can gain valuable experience that will increase your awareness ready for a time when there is something larger at stake and you will be able to make a decision that will keep you focused on your true goals.

Energizing Visualization and Affirmation Through Meditation

There are many different self-help systems around today that advocate the use of visualization, positive thinking and affirmation as tools for attaining your goals. These tools are generally useful to have in your 'self-help arsenal' but unless they are connected to the three energies of the body, mind and spirit they will be rendered more or less impotent. When implementing visualization, affirmation or, in fact, prayer (which is one of the earliest forms of visualization), most people will tend to repeat a phrase or two and maybe try to hold a picture in their 'mind's eye' – the more diligent might actually write down their goals on a piece of paper (Bruce Lee affirmed his future movie-star status by writing it down). All of these methods tend to use only a small part of the potential energy stored in the body. However, if you connect, through the process of Meditation, to the whole of your presence and then implement your visualization, affirmation or prayer then it will have a lot more power and influence in your life. This is because not only will you use the power of your mind (through reading the words or seeing a picture) to energize it, but you will also feel the affirmation and sense it in your body. For example, you may see yourself in your mind's eye doing a great interview but through Meditation you can also feel what it would be like to do a great interview and actually sense the gestures and body language that you would actually be using. In this way, your vision for the interview is programmed into your subconscious mind through multiple channels and your subconscious mind will then help you to make your vision a reality.

An Intelligent Warrior knows and accepts that although visualization and positive thought are useful it is naïve to think that just because you visualize something it is going to immediately come about (as many self-help books would like to have you think). The fact is, you may have to 'fight' for some time and employ a continual stream of instructions to your subconscious before the Action/Reaction Cycle is affected enough and your inner wish is 'born' fully into the outer world. The main reason why so many positive intentions fall by the wayside or even seemingly bring about the opposite of what was originally intended is that 'visualizers' lack a robust enough connection to the energies within them to stay the distance required; this is characterized by a lack of patience and perseverance. It stands to reason that if you connect more deeply to yourself through the process of Meditation, when you give yourself an affirmation it will also travel more deeply into your subconscious mind and consequently have more influence on your life.

How To Unlock the Wisdom of Our Mistakes

As your education has probably drummed into you from the year dot that getting an answer wrong is bad and that generally you are bad and/or stupid if you make a mistake, you probably do not unlock all of the wisdom available to you from your mistakes. Making mistakes is very much like the experience of pain in that we want to avoid it at all costs, yet pain alerts us to problems in our body, mind and spirit that need our attention. In much the same way, mistakes teach us where we are going wrong in the pursuit of our aims; moreover, with the correct attitude getting something 'wrong' usually teaches us far more than getting something right. In this light, the biggest mistake that we can make is, in fact, ignoring our mistakes. It has been said that the definition of insanity is doing the same thing repeatedly but expecting different results. It is also true that a passenger jet flies off course 90 per cent of the time but the onboard computer senses this and brings (re-balances) it repeatedly back on course until it reaches its final intended destination. Most self-made millionaires have been penniless a few times and will often talk of the many failures it takes to make a success. Making mistakes is an essential part of life and forms a balancing complementary force to our experiences of success. The key to unlocking the wisdom held in your mistakes lies in the Action/Reaction Cycle. When you become aware of a mistake, either by your own insight or by somebody informing you of it, it is imperative that you open yourself to it and allow it to be assimilated via your senses by your brain. This helps the brain to compare the balance between action and reaction and modify its response in order to attain a different result next time that is hopefully more in keeping with what you intended. This response is expressed or manifested via your body, for instance, instead of saying 'yes' you try a different approach and say 'no', and so the cycle continues as you then perceive the effect that this has had on the situation in question.

The problems occur when you break this process and desensitize yourself to the effect you are having in the outside world because you do not want to admit that you have made a mistake; this is largely the realm of your ego because it does not give up its image of you easily and has a tendency to think that it knows everything.

An Intelligent Warrior needs to turn and face their mistakes, learn from them and embrace the fact that they do not know; this opens up the possibility to gather more information and experience in order to be able to make a more appropriate decision next time. Also in this way, we can free ourselves from the debilitating effects of embarrassment, which is caused by our projection of people judging us negatively.

Reacquainting Yourself With the Power of instinct

Westerners have become increasingly divorced from the instinctual power inherent in the body. Their continual rape and prostitution of the Earth, their pollution of the atmosphere, their insane tampering with their foodstuffs and their ridiculous conviction that they are somehow separate and superior to Mother Nature are some of the things that have dulled and anaesthetized their once virile powers of instinct. The Intelligent Warrior must work to reawaken these powers for they lie at the heart of holistic self-defence; we have an instinctual sense of balance, our bodies instinctively make thousands of decisions every second to keep our physiology in homeostasis and when we are under threat our instinct triggers the fight-or-flight response. Our instinct plays a large part in the development of intuitive thought, which is the pathway to a higher form of intelligence and communication possible for human beings; it can be experienced operating in our daily lives when we experience a 'gut reaction' to something or someone and at times of an inspired realization. Reawakening your instinct begins with the conscious direction of your attention into your own body, for it is here that our instinct originates and not from any abstraction in our mind. Through Meditation and Chi Kung the Intelligent Warrior begins to forge a deeper connection with their instinct and most importantly with the process of breathing, which as we have seen is one of the places where our conscious thought (somatic nervous system) can join with our instinctive functions (autonomic nervous system). Moreover, by turning and facing moments of fear, pain, anxiety and so on, the Intelligent Warrior gains valuable experience and insight into one of the only times that Westerners still experience their instinct, that is during the fight-or-flight response. Other things that can awaken your instinct are:

1 **Eating raw plant food.** *This society has now reached a level of overwhelming stupidity when it comes to the ingestion of physical food. We have now tampered with the vast majority of everything that we put in our mouths. Through the processes of cooking, refining, processing, 'enhancing' and the unbelievably insane genetic 'modification', we have slowly 'denatured' our foodstuffs and so divorced ourselves further from our true natural origins. Eating raw plant food, especially if it is wild, provides a feast of minerals, nutrients, enzymes and vitamins in perfect balance that has been created by our creator, nature herself. The moment food is tampered with by a lesser intelligence this balance is lost and with it a higher form of nourishment.*

2 **Spend time in nature.** *If you live in the city, this is something that you may have to fight for and spend some of your hard-earned cash on. Surrounding yourself in a natural environment is raw food for the senses and, through the Principle of Resonation, the ingestion of this food begins to awaken our instinct and the awesome experience of being at one with nature.*

3 **Limit the amount of time you spend exposed to electricity and electromagnetic waves.** *The Intelligent Warrior must adapt to any environment they find themselves surrounded by. In modern society, the presence of electromagnetic waves is an inescapable*

part of life but, as they tend to disrupt the finer electrical fields that emanate from your body, you must take steps to protect yourself. The best way to strengthen and rebalance your energy fields is through practising Chi Kung.

Developing Efficient Time Management

Time management is a valuable skill in modern society and takes a surprising amount of discipline in times of stress. The only place where true time management can take place is from the present moment, for it is only here that we can do the following:

1 *See accurately into the future and predict how much time is necessary for a particular task.*
2 *Keep centred enough to be able to keep to our schedule in times of stress.*
3 *Be adaptable enough to change our schedule should the task require it.*

Time management plays a large part in holistic self-defence because we must make time on a regular basis to practise; you will need a clear head and a well-prepared schedule in order to do battle with the various excuses that parts of you will create to justify skipping your practise session!

Nurturing Your Creative Self

Because Western society places great emphasis on material status, many people find that the artistic sides of their being sometimes begin to atrophy from lack of stimulation. The body then tends to prompt us in various ways to feed our creative self. This nurturing could take the form of learning to play a musical instrument, painting or starting that novel you have been meaning to write for the last 10 years. The important point for the Intelligent Warrior is that this is another example of your body trying to re-establish its homeostasis. Creative endeavours are not just trivial hobbies as much of our society would like to believe, they are in fact a form of medicine for the integration of your body, mind and spirit. Because we have had certain attitudes bred into us, an Intelligent Warrior will have to feed and protect their creative self and ensure that the soldiers of cynicism, negativity and the fear of failure do not wound it. Traditionally in Kung Fu schools artistic skills such as calligraphy and music were taught hand in hand with martial skills for the Masters realized that true strength comes from finding and strengthening a balanced relationship between body, mind and spirit. Because your creative self deals with your self-expression it can lay you open to wounds at an emotional level – this fear of pain can often stunt the growth of our creative self and sometimes kill it outright. The wounds can come from both without and within, for instance, you perhaps paint a picture, which you found to be an enriching and enjoyable experience so you decide to show it to a friend who then laughs at it and says his dog could do better. The pain of this then triggers negative internal conversation within you and you start telling yourself that you will never amount to anything as a painter so you might as well just give up. This is a fairly simplistic example and in reality the wounding putdowns from both within and without can be much more subtle and applied over a long period of time (such as happens in many long-term relationships where one partner engages in artistic endeavour and the other does not). Once again your awareness and presence are powerful weapons against this form of attack, your awareness alerting you to the fact that you are being hurt and your presence then being brought to bear on the situation, perhaps utilizing nonattachment and then reaffirming your goals.

The Precious Moments of inspiration

On a more cheerful note, there are times when we stand before something of a truly inspirational nature such as a work of art, a piece of music, a beautiful flower or a starlit night. These moments are something to be valued above all others and especially above the desire to own or have 'things'; they open us to another level of life. An artist communicates their sensitivity (gained by hours of discipline) through their chosen medium, we receive their communication via our senses and our body reacts by filling us with the potential of another way of seeing, sometimes bringing out feelings of inadequacy and/or humility, sometimes eliciting a joy that brings tears to our eyes. These moments are truly life affirming and we do not want to forget them easily. The process of opening, outlined in Meditation, can allow you in these situations to facilitate the entry of these impressions into yourself at a deep level for they are for the most part experiences and not words (although words can awaken a feeling of inspiration).

How to Stop Difficult Decisions from Driving You insane

Difficult decisions always tend to split our minds into the proverbial 'Yes' and 'No'. If our mind is not clear then we continually bounce between these two, imagining the various outcomes of our decision.

We therefore very often paralyse our self and cannot make a decision with the weight of our conviction behind it and then, when we do make a decision, we torture ourselves wondering whether it was the right one. This can be very detrimental to our mental health and in situations where people are looking to us for direction and leadership. If you find yourself in this dilemma, use Meditation to clear your mind, relax your body and calm your emotions. Meditate on the fact that right and wrong are part of the same whole, and that any decision you make just brings different results and moreover an Intelligent Warrior will learn and grow from the experience.

PROTECT YOURSELF FROM NEGATIVITY DUE TO CHEMICAL IMBALANCE

It is imperative for the Intelligent Warrior to understand when an actual physical substance is affecting their psychophysical balance. The following is a list of some of the most common:

1 **Hangovers.** *These tend to generate negative thoughts and feelings. Remind yourself that you are feeling and thinking this way because of a chemical imbalance brought about by the ingestion of alcohol.*

2 **Comedowns from harder drugs.** *These usually generate more intense negative thoughts and feelings than hangovers do. If you are a hard-drug user then familiarize yourself with the 'comedown pattern' of any drug that you use on a regular basis. This will allow your mind to combat any paranoia and depression by again understanding that it is a chemical imbalance that is creating the negative emotional states and will give you confidence in your body's miraculous ability to rebalance itself.*

3 **Getting hungry.** *The expression of our negative emotions is held*

in check by a certain amount of energy. When this energy depletes, such as when we get hungry, there is a tendency for us to express these negative emotions.

4 **Getting tired.** This is very similar to being hungry.

5 **Lack of natural sunlight.** The sun provides us with the most vital energy that we need so if we are deprived of it then lethargy and depression will soon follow.

6 **The consumption of refined sugar.** Unbelievably, refined sugar is one of the most dangerous drugs in society. Because it is highly addictive and has a severe impact on your body's blood-sugar levels (balance), it can create very bad emotional habits, especially in children. Get rid of it as much as possible from your diet, read some literature on its effects and protect your children from it.

7 **Smoking.** I will not bore you with the usual facts about how bad smoking is; however, even when people know the devastating effects that smoking has on our health they do not stop smoking (Incidentally, most cigarettes are cured with a form of sugar to make them more addictive.) Smoking severely depletes Chi levels by disrupting the body's CO_2/O_2 balance, which in turn severely impairs the body's ability to heal itself and lays it open to attack from negative thoughts and emotional states (this is also due to the part of the brain that is affected by smoking).

Your awareness and presence are your most powerful tools against negative states triggered by chemical imbalances in the body and if you familiarize yourself with the types of things that throw yourself out of balance then you will be able to lessen their impact on your general homeostasis.

DEFENDING (YOURSELF) AGAINST ADDICTIONS

Addictions offer us the opportunity to see the different sides of ourselves go to war. For example, one 'person' in us wants to be healthy and decides that we will not eat any more chocolate; thus we start the day intending to carry out this aim. However, by the afternoon we are feeling a bit tired after a stressful morning and the other 'person' in us starts to argue that, because we are tired we need a bit of a boost, and, that as we have worked hard, we deserve a reward. From this point on these two different 'people' argue inside our heads until one gives way and we decide on a course of action. The main theatre that this battle is played out in is in our heads, in the form of internal conversation. However, this quickly transfers into the emotional part of ourselves bringing feelings of self-righteousness, guilt or anxiety to the fore, and soon afterwards manifests itself as tension in the physical body. In the meantime, we have burnt a substantial amount of energy and not paid as much attention as we could have to the present task in hand.

We can become addicted, in varying degrees of intensity, to anything; food, television, sleep, sex, danger, drugs, fighting, computers, jogging and celebrities all hold their own particular allure. The answer to fighting addiction lies in a familiar place: a sense of balance. As we have seen from our studies, only in the present moment can we truly embrace the Yes and the No, the Yin and the Yang. And only when we have developed a presence strong enough to stand in between these two poles and hold them equally in each hand will we ever gain an insight into our true nature. Our strength lies not in denying one thing or the other but in our ability to see that we are not one person. With this acceptance comes compassion for others and ourselves and the ability to integrate. We begin to watch as the continual interplay of Yin and Yang dances in and around us to a rhythm whose origins we can only begin to under-stand via a movement into the present moment. The doorway to this kind of understanding lies in the connection to your own body, for it is here that many of the mysteries of our meaning lie. The battle against addiction can be one of life and death and our decisions can kill us – maybe today (an accident), maybe tomorrow (through disease). Your responsibility as an Intelligent Warrior is to remember death and know that unless you are consciously seeking life, the experience of which is communicated to you through your body, then disease and ultimately death are not far away. This may seem a little extreme, but only the force of this kind of remembrance will ever have the strength to sever the ties between your true self and addiction.

Over the course of this book it has been stressed over and over again that you must struggle to develop somebody in the centre of your being who can see and sense directly the expansion and contraction, the Yin and the Yang, that is the language of life, always fluctuating and always moving in balance and rebalance. Nothing in life is stagnant, it is evolving up or involving down; everything that you see around you will one day return to the earth as dust – every house, every car and every person will one day cease to be. The life of the universe operates on a level that we cannot comprehend – cycles upon cycles for millions of years. It is not surprising that we find it hard to comprehend the fact that if the life of our planet was a 24-hour day then we will have only been alive for two seconds. Yet our life, though insignificant when seen on this scale, has a place and a definite role or destiny to 'fulfil', of that you can be sure. Therefore, we begin the process of listening and opening in the hope that we may come to understand what our response-ability truly means in the face of this exquisite scale. In order to do this, we must first make the decision to harmonize the warring within ourselves to stop the

The Intelligent Warrior

disintegration brought about by our fears, which divide us first into two and then into many. The Intelligent Warrior must work diligently to bring communication between his body, mind and spirit so as to 'be-come' one in accordance with a fundamental law that permeates the universe: the 'law of three', which encompasses positive, negative and neutralizing forces. Know also that in doing this you will be strengthening those around you and in doing so, strengthening the planet, which helps the planet to face the countless attacks that modern man inflicts upon it every day. Perhaps by listening and becoming 'in tune' with the planet we may begin to understand the hierarchy it belongs to and what responsibility it must fulfil, but for now we return to a sense of breath, our feet on the ground, for this is where our work lies, and we can decide at any moment to turn in that direction. I wish you all, from the depth of my being, true courage in pursuit of this.

in closing

The exercises in this book are not really exercises at all, they are snapshots of life. Some will find resonance with you, others will not. At the end of the day, they should be viewed as a starting point. I urge you to find areas in your life where fear and its related emotions operate and, once your awareness becomes attuned to the sensations of fear, and your presence finds its way into your life, you will be able to make decisions that will guide you towards homeostasis. You will then be able to identify more clearly the changes you need to make in order to fulfil your deepest wishes. I know that this is a big promise, but the actual material for transforming your life is with you every second, it is only the connection, the seeing, the sensing, that you need to find; and that process can begin right now with the sensation of your breathing, your hand on the book ...

references

Casteneda, Carlos (1971) *A Separate Reality*, Penguin.

Castaneda, Carlos (1972) *Journey to Ixtlan*, Penguin.

Chaitow, Leon, Bradley, Diana and Gilbert, Christopher (2002) *Multidisciplinary Approaches to Breathing Pattern Disorders*, Harcourt Publishers.

Gurdjieff, G.I. (1976) *Views from the Real World*, Routledge & Kegan Paul.

Keeley, Graham (2003) 'Muggers Kicked Me in the Head for £50', *Evening Standard*, 24 September.

Lee, Bruce (1975) *The Tao of Jeet Kune Do*, Ohara Publications.

Lee, Bruce (1997) *The Tao of Gung Fu*, Tuttle.

Lusseyran, Jacques (1999) *What One Sees Without Eyes*, trans. Rob Baker, Parabola Books.

Ming, Shi and Weijia, Siao (1994) *Mind Over Matter*, trans. Thomas Cleary, Frog Ltd.

Tzu, Sun (1988) *The Art of War*, trans. Thomas Cleary, Shambala
  Publications (originally written *c.* 600 BC).
Vithoulkas, George (1986) *The Science of Homeopathy*, Thorsons.

further reading

Arlin, Dini and Wolfe, *Nature's First Law: The Raw Food Diet*, Maul Brothers Publishing.

Bentov, Itzhak (1979) *Stalking the Wild Pendulum*, Fontana.

Gurdjieff, G.I. (1971) *Meetings with Remarkable Men,* trans A. R. Oragen, Routledge & Kegan Paul.

Laozi (1997) *The Tao of Power* trans R. L. Wing, Thorsons.

Jeffers, Susan (1987) *Feel the Fear and Do It Anyway*, Arrow Books.

Ouspensky, P. D. (1975) *In Search of the Miraculous*, Routledge & Kegan Paul.

Thomas, Bruce (2002) *Bruce Lee Fighting Spirit*, Sidgwick and Jackson.

Thomas, Bruce (2003) *Bruce Lee Fighting Talk,* Bentwyck Henry Publishers.

Thompson, Geoff (2001) *Watch My Back,* Summersdale.

Index

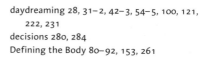